Leo Butler
Plays: 1

Made of Stone, Redundant, Lucky Dog, The Early Bird

Made of Stone: 'Set in Northern England, and written in a blaze of fury, with emotions bouncing off the walls like whacking great billiard balls, the play is both a howl of rage and an acute examination of the individual roots of macho posturing and racist attitudes. Featuring one of the most excruciating scenes of teenage sex ever staged, and some very troubling emotions, this working-class drama ends on a tentative note of hope.' *What's on in London*

Redundant: 'Butler boldly creates a psychologically complex female lead. He also looks to be a master of stagecraft, subtly manipulating his audience and characters with dramatic reversals, before arriving at an ending that is inevitable, surprising and loaded with pity and fear.' *Evening Standard*
'Written with gobsmacking psychological realism – Butler's text is full of evasions, projections and concealed aggression – this scorching drama is raw, raucous and disturbing, with a final stage picture of almost intolerable bleakness.' *Stage*

Lucky Dog: 'A darkly funny and remarkably poignant portrait of a marriage. Butler's dialogue combines naturalistic chat, a musical sense of phrase and pause, and surreal episodes. The last act is an extraordinary *coup de théâtre*, imbued with an almost heavenly sense of new-found tenderness and atonement.' *Independent on Sunday*
'Butler reveals himself as a writer of prescience and subtlety. It's a play that stays with you.' *Independent*

The Early Bird: 'The stage is filled with unspoken terror in this haunting, hypnotic drama. When the curtain falls you want to look away quickly, and head back into the light.' *Belfast Telegraph*

Leo Butler was born in Sheffield in 1974. His first play, *Made of Stone*, was produced as part of the Royal Court Theatre Young Writers' Festival in 2000. His other plays include *Redundant* (Royal Court Downstairs, 2001), winner of the George Devine Award for Most Promising Playwright; *Lucky Dog* (Royal Court Upstairs, 2004), and *The Early Bird* (Queens Theatre, Belfast, 2006), produced by Ransom Productions as part of the Belfast Festival. Other work includes two war plays for teenagers, *Devotion* (Theatre Centre, London, 2002) and *Heroes* (National Theatre, 2007), and *I'll Be the Devil* (Tricycle Theatre, London, 2008), produced by the Royal Shakespeare Company. Leo Butler lives in London with his wife and daughter.

LEO BUTLER

Plays: 1

Made of Stone
Redundant
Lucky Dog
The Early Bird

with an introduction by the author

Methuen Drama

METHUEN DRAMA CONTEMPORARY DRAMATISTS

1 3 5 7 9 10 8 6 4 2

This collection first published in Great Britain in 2008 by Methuen Drama

Methuen Drama
A & C Black Publishers Limited
38 Soho Square
London W1D 3HB
www.acblack.com

Made of Stone first published by Methuen Drama in 2008
Copyright © 2008 by Leo Butler
Redundant first published by Methuen Publishing in 2001
Copyright © 2001 by Leo Butler
Lucky Dog first published by Methuen Publishing in 2004
Copyright © 2004 by Leo Butler
The Early Bird first published by Methuen Drama in 2006
Copyright © 2006 by Leo Butler
Introduction © 2007 by Leo Butler

Leo Butler has asserted his rights under the Copyright, Designs and Patents Act, 1988, to be
identified as the author of these works

ISBN: 978 1 4081 0147 6

A CIP catalogue record for this book is available from the British Library

Typeset by SX Composing DTP, Rayleigh, Essex
Printed and bound in Great Britain by Cox & Wyman, Reading, Berkshire

Contents

Leo Butler
Chronology

2000   *Made of Stone* premiered at the Royal Court Theatre
       Upstairs, London, as part of the Young Writers
       Festival

2001   *Redundant* premiered at the Royal Court Theatre
       Downstairs and won the George Devine Award for
       Most Promising Playwright

2002   *Devotion* premiered at the Theatre Centre, London,
       directed by Liam Steel

2004   *Lucky Dog* premiered at the Royal Court Theatre
       Upstairs

2006   *The Early Bird* produced by Ransom Productions and
       premiered at the Queen's Theatre, Belfast, as part of
       the Belfast Festival

2007   *Heroes* directed by Samantha Potter and toured to
       London schools by the National Theatre's Education
       Department

2007   *Airbag* presented at the Royal Court Theatre Upstairs
       as part of the Rough Cuts season in collaboration
       with Nigerian choreographer Odey Anthony

2008   *I'll Be the Devil* produced by the Royal Shakespeare
       Company and premiered at the Tricycle Theatre,
       London

Introduction

All four plays in this volume began with an image, or stage picture, that came to me by chance. For *Made of Stone* it was the image of two brothers standing at their father's graveside, while *The Early Bird* began with the image of a couple sitting together on stage, facing an unseen interrogator. For *Lucky Dog* it was the image of a woman turning into a dog and barking at her husband, and for *Redundant* it was a teenage girl pushing a pram in circles on the stage – a kind of contemporary Mother Courage, relocated to a Sheffield council estate. Although this particular image never made it to the play, it did lead me to the central character and helped me form the play's structure.

Along with an image, and before I write a word of dialogue, I almost always have the play's title. *Made of Stone*, for instance, is a tribute to the Stone Roses' song of the same name, *Redundant* was lifted directly from a quote in Nick Davies's book *Dark Heart*, and *Lucky Dog*, from the moment it came to me (almost a year before I wrote it), just sounded right. Indeed, there were many different versions of *Lucky Dog* before the one that was produced. There was a play about ageing rockers set in Woolwich Arsenal, a comedy set in Benidorm, and a play about a serial killer set in Blackpool. Each play was worlds apart from the one eventually staged, but they all featured characters called Eddie and Sue, and they each shared a moment when a woman turns into a dog and barks at her husband. Over six months or more, I wrote hundreds of pages of material, creating set-ups that had no life beyond their initial twenty or thirty pages. It wasn't until I forced myself to admit what it was that I really wanted to write that *Lucky Dog* quickly and organically began to crystallise. The story of a couple whose children have left home, and who are subsequently forced to question whether they still love each other, may not sound that interesting on the page, but it resonated with me and, choosing to set it over Christmas Day, gave me a focus that allowed me to complete the first draft in a matter of days. The wife's metamorphosis into the dog suddenly found a context, and gave me a fitting climax to work towards, while fragments from my previous attempts, most notably the Benidorm play, suddenly found a home.

The first draft, for me, is almost always about finding the narrative, and, in this search, I try not to dwell on the play's argument or meaning. Whether the play has any meaning beyond the narrative is something I'd rather think about later, through subsequent drafts, through try-outs and rehearsals, or even right up until performance. There have been times when from the outset I was certain of the play's supposed 'message', only to find that I had written something entirely different by the end. When *Lucky Dog* was later staged in Budapest, there were many in the audience who commented that what they had seen was a direct metaphor for the state of their country in the wake of the Cold War. Which, of course, it is. For other people it is also a simple story of the breakdown, and eventual transformation, of a marriage, or a meditation on the conflict between love and the necessity of companionship, while to other audiences it might be no more than a long and uncomfortable night out at the theatre. It really doesn't matter. The play has its own meaning for me, which itself can change from performance to performance, and I would prefer that the audience came to its own conclusions anyway. I think it keeps the play alive somehow.

Produced by the Royal Court in 2004, *Lucky Dog* was beautifully directed by James Macdonald. One of the show's highlights came right at the end of the play, when the back wall collapsed, revealing the fluorescent yellow beach on which stood Linda Bassett (who only moments before had been snarling and barking), a transformed woman in her bathing suit and shades. This wonderful scene change was one of those rare occasions when the combined talents of the company come together and create a moment of pure theatrical magic.

In the summer of 2000 I had already submitted a couple of plays for the Royal Court's biannual Young Writers'

Festival, but – with only a month until the submission deadline – I knew I could and should write a third. Having decided on the title, and with the image of the two brothers standing by their father's grave, I locked myself away and wrote the first draft of *Made of Stone* from start to finish, working out the characters and plot as I went along. It differed from the other plays I had submitted because – perhaps for the first time – I was writing truthfully about a world and people I knew and cared for. Looking back on it now, it has an exuberance and energy – some might say naïveté – that only a debut play can have.

Though it is not autobiographical, *Made of Stone* is one of my most personal plays and is, in some ways, a love letter to the city and to the people of Sheffield. As I worked through the first draft I soon realised that I was writing about families, particularly working-class families, who, at the cusp of the millennium, are struggling to identify their own particular place in the world. The death of the father became a potent and appropriate way of articulating this, and Gary's temptation to migrate to London and Miles's latent bigotry are just a couple of the symptoms that come out of this dilemma. However, for all its intentions, the play works best as a simple and emotional story of a family coming to terms with bereavement. It was directed by Deborah Bruce and I think there are moments in *Made of Stone* that I have never bettered, and it was a joy to see them come alive, particularly those scenes – the teenage sex scene, for example – that were performed exactly as I had imagined them.

Following the Young Writers' Festival, Graham Whybrow and Ian Rickson (the Royal Court's literary and artistic directors at that time) invited me to come and work at the theatre as a writer-on-attachment. It was an eight-week stint during which I was shut away in one of the offices and left alone to write. It was here that, working continuously through the day, and often through the night, I finished the first draft of *Redundant*. Having both an image, a possible central character, and, of course, the title, I experimented with various scenes and starting points. The

first scene of the play was written in a notebook in the
theatre bar, which I then quickly typed up back in the office.
The central character, Lucy – inspired by a small number of
girls I knew when I was a teenager – leapt off the page at
me, and her situation, it seemed, had a lot of dramatic
potential. I then imagined, given the circumstances set up in
the first scene, what would happen if we followed a year in
the teenage girl's life. This gave the play a cyclical structure,
and its episodic form, which served to highlight Lucy's
tragic journey as she makes one terrible decision after
another, regardless of the consequences. Though she is a
product of her society and very much a victim of poverty –
in particular, poverty of imagination and of opportunity –
Lucy is, in contrast, never a victim in her own home. Both
in the text and in the subsequent production, Lucy's flat
becomes a kind of doll's house, or a play-pen for a girl who
is without parents, has never had the chance to grow up, but
who is nevertheless trapped in an adult world, taking refuge
in fantasy. Though her circumstances take a downward
spiral, Lucy – and this is what attracted me to her in the first
place – never gives up, and both her dreams, however
delusional, and her tough, oppositional spirit remain
unspoiled (for right or for wrong) even by the end of the
play.

It was a joy to write and there were times when the
dialogue simply spilled out on to the page, leaving me with
very little work to do. Of course, there were subsequent
drafts which I developed, in dialogue with Graham and
director Dominic Cooke, over a period of months. But
rewriting, at its best, should always serve the initial idea and
that first burst of text. Thankfully, the Royal Court are
pretty good with playwrights, and, in any case, I always
know when I'm cheating.

There is a line in *Redundant* where the gran says,
'Someone should bomb this bloody country. That'd wake us
up a bit. Saddam Hussein or someone. IRA, bleedin'
whatsisface? Bin Laden. Yeah, he could do it. Drop a few
tons of anthrax. Teach us what it really means to suffer.'
The play's press night was on 12 September 2001, and it

was produced in the Theatre Downstairs. It is the first play in history to mention Osama Bin Laden, and there was some suspicion that I deliberately added the line to court controversy, though this wasn't the case at all. Though the line is written almost as a throwaway aside to the audience, it was intended as a deliberate means of revealing the extent of the grandmother's disillusion with the world around her, as opposed to the cheap shock tactic which it was accused of being. By the time of the press night, we had kept the line, but removed the Bin Laden reference, but the gesture alone was enough to send a collective gasp over the theatre – more so, in fact, than the battering of the grandmother that followed it. Dominic directed a brilliant production, and Lyndsey Marshal gave an excellent performance as Lucy. However, this didn't stop many of the critics savaging the play, and it was, with a few exceptions, a critical flop, and a commercial disaster for the theatre.

The title of the play might have had a part in this, and it was marketed as an austere and bleak chamber piece, without any hint of the play's comedy. But it was the attacks on the Twin Towers that really, and unsurprisingly, turned audiences and critics away. Thankfully, for many who did see it, *Redundant* did have an impact and I will always look back on the production as one of both enormous fun and of great personal importance. Although when it came to *Lucky Dog*, produced in May of 2004, there was more than a sense of dread when the husband declares that the Queen will be dead 'come summer'.

Redundant is, in some ways, a companion piece to *Made of Stone*, in that they both deal with children who live in a world without adults. Likewise, *The Early Bird* is, in some ways, a companion piece to *Lucky Dog* because both plays share an intimate and claustrophobic form, and, significantly, deal with adults who live in a world without children. But while the child in *Lucky Dog* has simply grown up and left home, the girl in *The Early Bird* has suddenly, and without explanation, vanished into thin air. The girl's parents struggle to reason with the suddenness of her apparent death, and when all attempts at consolation turn

to blame, the mother can find solace only in her horrific
fantasies.

It was written for Ransom Productions, who are based in
Belfast and led by Rachel O'Riordan, the company's
director. The play also marks my first departure from the
familiar setting of Sheffield, but, like its predecessors, it was
written in a burst of energy born out of dogged
determination to get to the end, whatever that might be.
The story flips backwards and forwards in time, without any
scene change, and at times the form deliberately obscures
the play's logic, as indeed the event has obscured Jack and
Debbie's own reasoning. The conviction that – unlike a lot
of contemporary drama – life operates by chance, rather
than out of any logical or moral order, weighs heavily on
The Early Bird, which is why it is such a heavy and upsetting
play. But, for me, the characters' ultimate descent into
fantasy does reveal a peculiar kind of redemption, and, most
importantly, one of human choice.

I'd like to thank all the artists and practitioners who have
inspired and supported me with the four plays in this
volume. Particular thanks go to Graham Whybrow, Ian
Rickson, Dominic Cooke, James Macdonald, Ola
Animashawun and all the team (past and present) at the
YWP.

Many thanks also to Willy Russell.

I am indebted to my friends and family, especially my
parents, for all their love and encouragement.

Finally, I would like to thank my beautiful wife, Nazzi, for
being my very favourite critic, and for kicking me up the
arse when I need it most.

Leo Butler
2007

Made of Stone

Made of Stone was first performed at the Royal Court Theatre Upstairs, as part of the Young Writers' Festival, on 13 October 2000. The cast was as follows:

Elaine	Joanna Bacon
Gary	Nick Moss
Miles	Giles Ford
Pete	Greg Chisholm
Errol	Huss Garbiya
Carol	Sarah Cattle

Directed by Deborah Bruce
Designed by Liz Cooke
Lighting by Marion Mahon
Sound by Rich Walsh

Characters

Elaine, *early fifties, mother to three sons, white*
Gary, *thirty years old*
Miles, *twenty-eight years old*
Pete, *twenty-one years old*
Errol, *twenty-eight years old, black*
Carol, *sixteen years old*

Setting

Autumn, 2000. In and around Sheffield, South Yorkshire.
The play spans four weeks.

Scene One

Graveyard. Day.

Gary *and* **Pete** *standing before gravestone. They smoke cigarettes.*

Gary Seems like only yesterday dunt it? Shame about the birdshit.

Pete Too small anyway.

Gary Did yer bring any flowers or owt?

Pause.

Gary Me neither.

Pete Needs a tree. Should o'put 'im under tree over there. Too crowded 'ere.

Gary Don't be daft. 'E'll just be bones by now.

Pete Dunt make it right though.

Long pause.

Gary I told 'im we were comin'. Miles, I mean.

Pete Did yer?

Gary He's got a job. Down some buildin' site.

Pete Why'd you come?

Gary 'Cause. Pay me respect. Keep yer company.

Pete What about Mum?

Gary Dint ask.

Long pause.

Gary She's dyed 'er 'air blonde.

Pete What?

Gary Mum. She's dyed 'er 'air blonde.

Long pause.

Yer should go n'see 'er, Pete. I'm worried about 'er.

Pete   'E never did like crowds did 'e?

Gary   Man's dead, Pete.

Pete   If it'd been up to me, I'd've put 'im in backyard. Next t'shed. Can still 'ear 'im, yer know? In me 'ead. Talks to me when I'm asleep.

Gary   F'fucksake, Pete. It's been over a year now. Gotta start thinkin' of yerself. Never even see yer no more.

Pete   'E give us a rabbit other night. I were runnin' through this forest, down tracks like, in me dream. Next thing I know he's stood there, by the stream, with this rabbit in 'is arms. I tried to say somert, but yer know when yer open yer mouth n'the words don't come no matter 'ow 'ard yer try? Like yer've just swallowed glue or somert, stuck in back o'yer throat. That's what it were like. But 'e just stares at me, dead fuckin' serious n'e puts this rabbit by me feet, on mud. Dint run off or nothin', the rabbit. Just sat there. So, I picked it up. Wi' me dad just watchin' in that suit 'e used to wear for work. Ash stains on legs.

Long pause.

Gary   It's over, Pete. Come on. We all knew it were gonna happen sooner or later. 'E wunt want to see yer like this.

Long pause.

Look. Yer thought any more 'bout what I said? Movin' in wi' me n'Mum. It'd do yer good. Even if it's just forra bit. Yer know? Get yer feet back on ground.

Pete   Don't give a shit do yer?

Gary   Eh? 'Course I bloody do.

Pete   I came 'ere forra reason, yer don't 'ave to stay. Yer dint 'ave to come at all. And no, I'm not movin' in with you n' Mum. 'Appy where I am thanks.

Gary That shitty little bedsit? Fuckin' can't see walls f'damp. Yer can't even afford it, Pete.

Pete I'm workin' aren't I?

Gary Two nights a week int workin', mate.

Pete At least I've got a fuckin' job.

Gary Don't tell me yer blowin' it all.

Pete What?

Gary The cash 'e left yer. Well?

Long pause.

Look, just think about it, OK? Yer can even 'ave my room if yer want.

Long pause.

Pete Think I'll bring a cloth next time. Cloth n'a bucket.

Gary I'm leavin', Pete. I'm gettin' out of 'ere.

Pete Clean 'im up f'winter. Once birds've gone.

Gary Dint you 'ear me? I said I'm goin'. I'm movin' to London. September. I've applied f'college down there.

Long pause.

Can't stay at Mum's all me life can I?

Pete I'm not goin' nowhere me.

Scene Two

Pub. Evening. Music.

Miles *and* **Errol** *play pool.*

Carol *sits at a table, a distance apart, drinking and smoking, her large rucksack by her feet.*

Miles Honest to God, Errol, yer wunt believe it.

Errol   Serious?

Miles   Fuckin' fanny everywhere.

Errol   What, down University like?

Miles   Union n'that. By the interchange.

Errol   Mandela Centre.

Miles   That's the one. Proper shit'ole init? Went down there Friday, just f'buzz like. Me n'Stevie Cyclops, yeah? You know Cyclops init? Used to 'ang about Abbeyfield on 'is bike? Twitchy little fucker with the lazy eye.

Errol   Right.

Miles   Fuckin' works in W H Smith's now.

Errol   No.

Miles   See 'im all the time. Fuckin' psycho on the sly. Used to be a gas sniffer n'that.

Errol   You went this student bar?

Miles   Just blagged it init? Said we were art students.

Errol   Well yer've got to.

Miles   Name o'game. Anyway, we got in, right? Fuckin' place is bangin' with all that techno shite, yer know? Bung-bung-bung-bung-bung-bung-bung-bung. I mean, f'fucksake! Thought I was in an arcade at first. Fuckin' Jet Set Willy. Like, where's the joystick, know what I mean? Gotta be off yer 'ead to listen to that crap – ooh, nice shot, Errol – but we stuck with it, right? Few drinks n'that. Cunt believe it. All these college birds lovin' it up in their fuckin' hot pants n'boob tubes n'shit. Dint know where to look. Thought I were gonna shoot me load there n'then. 'Ad to tuck me chopper under us belt like. This one girl, right? Arse like a Guatamolian peach.

Errol   Yeah?

Miles   Fuckin' fit as fuck, I swear! Tits out 'ere. Proper
kettledrums.

Errol   No.

Miles   She were only tiny n'all. Stunnin' features. Short
blonde 'air, like whatsit? Zoe Ball n'that, only with these tits.
So me n'Cyclops, yeah? Move in there all smooth like.
Fuckin' start dancin' with 'er, know what I mean? Well.
Never known owt like it.

Errol   What, she was up for it then?

Miles   Little thing starts pressin' up against us init? Three
of us on the dancefloor, right? He had 'er round the front, I
was round the back. There she was, just givin' it fuckin'
banga-banga, rubbin' it up against me wood. Now normally
yer'd just assume, cock-teasing little bitch, but she was like
sayin', 'I'm on for it, I'm on for it.' I mean, what's the sexiest
girl you can think of? Just off top of yer 'ead.

Errol   Erm . . .

Miles   Say Geri fuckin' Spice.

Errol   Yeah.

Miles   Imagine Geri spreads 'er legs for yer, right? Soppin'
fat ginger minge winkin' right at yer.

Errol   Right.

Miles *mimes having rampant sex on the pool table.*

Miles   FeeeaaaAANKAAA!!!

He laughs.

But yer would though wunt yer? Stands to reason.

Errol   And that's what this bird's like?

Miles   She'll fuck anything, Errol, I swear. Should o'been
there. Is it my shot?

Errol   What? Oh . . .

Miles   Thought it wa'.

He takes his shot.

Errol   Did yer do it then?

Miles   Eh?

Errol   With this girl n'that? Did yer . . . Yer know? Take 'er back n'that?

Miles   Ah, fuckin' . . . She was all over place by end o'night. Think 'er mates took 'er 'ome in a taxi or somert. Probably been neckin' load o'them E's n'that. Rot yer braincells them. We just went for kebabs n'that. Couple o'pornos back at Cyclops's place. Don't need women when yer've got yer mates do yer? Goin' out this Friday if yer interested. Down Kiki's n'that.

Errol   Can't. Goin' to me parents on Sunday. Bit of a roast like.

Miles   Oh? With the young 'un n'that?

Errol   Yeah. Don't really go out nowhere these days. Not now I'm . . . yer know?

Miles   Tied t'sink.

Errol   No. Just into me home comforts these days.

Miles   Arr. Watchin' the telly with the missis n'that.

Errol   Owt we fancy really. Gettin' into me cookin' as it goes. Been workin' wonders wi'me wok.

Miles   Fucksake, Errol.

Errol   What?

Miles   She'll 'ave you in tights next.

Errol   Bit o'give and take never 'urt no one. She's in Spain at the moment. Doin' a trainin' course. Wants to be one o'them tour guides.

Miles   All the more reason then. Live it up a bit. Swear to
God, come out wi'me n'Cyclops, yer won't know what's 'it
yer.

Errol   No. Not with the kid. Twenny-four-hour job in itself
that.

Miles   Must be 'ard. Kids n'that. I cunt do it. Not the
settlin' down type really. 'Ard enough lookin' after mesen,
never mind no . . . What's 'er name?

Errol   Claire?

Miles   No, the baby.

Errol   Nina. As in Nina Simone? The singer?

Miles   Oh, right. Must keep you up all night init? Cryin'
n'shittin' n'that.

Errol   No, she's quiet as a mouse once she's in crib. She's
beautiful. Fuckin' . . . Lights me up, yer know? Meks
everythin' seem worthwhile. All the crap yer put up with day
in, day out, she meks it all . . . Yer know?

Miles   Yeah.

Errol   Yer know?

Miles   I know.

Errol   Little bloody miracle she is.

Miles   Play yer bloody shot will yer?

Errol *takes his shot.*

Errol   Yer still livin' down Rock Street?

Miles   No, I'm in flats now. Hyde Park. Movin' up in
world. Fuckin' dump.

Errol   On yer own n'that?

Miles   Yeah.

Errol   Funny old world init?

Miles   Eh?

Errol   Last time I seen yer, yer were still wearin' corduroy fuckin' flares n'playin' bulldog in the park. You n'yer mates.

Miles   Ah, those were fuckin' days.

Errol   Right little terror you weren't yer?

Miles   Eh?

Errol   D'yer want another pint?

Miles   Oh . . .

Errol   What is it, bitter?

Miles   Go on then. Ta.

Errol   Yer know, I'm glad I bumped into you again. Was kinda dreadin' goin' back to the old site work. Yer know I 'ad me own business?

Miles   Really?

Errol   All the same stuff like. Plasterin', foundation repair, bit of artexin' 'ere n'there. Me n'me brother. Three years.

Miles   What happened?

Errol   Ah, all fell through dint it? Personal shit.

Miles   Shame.

Errol   Yeah, well. Back to basics now. Just gotta grit yer teeth n'bear it.

Miles   No point clingin' t'past.

Errol   No.

Errol   Bitter is it?

Miles   Cheers.

Exit **Errol**.

Pause.

Miles *picks up and chalks his cue.*

Enter **Pete**, *in uniform, collecting glasses. He passes* **Miles**, *without noticing him.*

Miles *pokes* **Pete** *up the arse with his cue.*

Miles   'Ey-'ey! Bet Lynch eat yer 'eart out!

Pete (*steadies himself*)   F''fucksake!

Miles   Shunt wiggle yer 'ips then should yer? Little tease.

Pete   When did you get 'ere?

Miles   'Bout to ask the same question.

Pete   Don't be causin' no trouble, Miles.

Miles   What?

Pete   You 'eard.

Miles   Come forra quiet drink, that's all. Been mixin' fuckin' plaster all day, I think I deserve it.

Pete   Just don't, all right? I know what yer like once yer've 'ad a few. Any excuse. You 'ant dragged Cyclops out 'ave yer?

Miles   No, just a guy from work. Black guy, looks like a crack'ead n'that. Fuckin' borin' the arse off me if yer really want to know. Goin' 'ome after this.

Pete   Good.

Pause. **Pete** *collects glasses,* **Miles** *breaks.*

Miles   'Eard yer went down graveyard wi' Gary.

Pause.

Miles   What's wrong? Can't yer speak to yer brother no more?

Pete *exits.*

Miles (*calls*)   Oh grow up, yer tosspot! What's wrong wi'yer?

Pete *re-enters with a cloth, wipes down* **Carol**'s *table.*

Miles   Sorry? Excuse me? . . . Hello? We are still related aren't we?

Pause.

Come on, Pete, I 'ant seen yer in ages.

Pause.

Oi! Don't ignore me! What's up with yer? 'Ave I upset yer or somert?

Pause.

Little fuckin' gobshite, 'ey!

Pete   D'yer want me to fetch the landlord?

Miles   What? And that's all yer can say? After how many weeks?

Pete   Look, just shut it, all right?

Miles   Is that a threat? Fuck me, so yer've got a bit o'sponk in yer after all. Give the boy an encore.

He starts applauding **Pete**.

Fuckin' star!

Pete   Look, just drink yer drink and fuck off, all right?

Miles (*stops clapping*)   Gotta hand it to yer Pete. Really know 'ow to make a man feel proud.

Pete   I'm not gonna argue with yer, Miles.

He makes to go.

Miles   Miserable little cunt. Get over it.

Pete (*stops, turns*)   What?

Miles   Before it's too late. 'E's dead, Pete. The bastard's . . .

Pete *throws the dirty cloth at* **Miles**'s *face.*

Pete   Don't you ever . . .

Miles   What?

Pete   . . . tell me . . .

Miles   Fuckin' startin'?

Pete   Just stay the fuck . . .

Miles   Come on then!

H hits **Pete** *with the snooker cue.*

Bastard!

Miles *and* **Pete** *fight.*

Miles   Fuckin' kill yer!

Enter **Errol** *with pints of bitter and crisps.*

Errol   Jesus!

Errol *puts the drinks down and gets in between* **Miles** *and* **Pete**, *pulling* **Miles** *away.*

What the . . . ? Miles!

Miles   Fuckin' cunt!

Errol   Miles!

Pete   Just stay away from me 'ere?!

Errol   What's goin' on? What's 'e said?

Pete   I'll do what the fuck I want, all right?! I don't need you, I don't . . .

Miles   I should fuckin' . . .

Pete   . . . need Gary, I don't need no one, 'ear?! No one!

Miles *breaks free from* **Errol**, *pushes* **Pete**, *who topples onto the floor.*

Miles   Yeah? Come on then!

Errol (*grabs Miles*)   Miles!

Miles (*pushes Errol*)   Get the fuck off me, will yer?!

Errol   What's goin' on?

Pause.

Miles?

Miles   Prick.

Miles *grabs his jacket and exits.*

Errol   Miles!

Errol *exits, chasing after* **Miles**.

Pete *pulls himself up off the floor.*

Carol   You all right? D'yer want an 'and?

Pause.

Thought 'e were gonna paste yer.

Pete   How old are you?

Carol   Old enough.

Scene Three

Elaine'*s flat. The kitchen. Evening.* **Gary** *sits at the table, staring at an opened letter.*

Pause.

Enter **Elaine**, *in a blue dress, made-up for a night out, carrying shoes. Faint music from the other room.*

Elaine   Oh, 'ello, petal. I didn't hear you come in.

She sits by the kitchen table and fixes on her shoes.

There's a pizza in the fridge if you want.

Gary   Yer goin' out?

Elaine   Oh, and a letter came for you this morning. I left it on the mantelpiece.

Gary   Yer goin' out drinkin' again aren't you?

Elaine   Well I'm hardly dressed for tennis am I?

She stands and twirls.

Well? What do you think? Yer'd hardly believe it was C&A would yer? Oh, I almost forgot.

She exits.

Gary   I thought we were going to watch the film tonight.

Elaine (*off*)   What?

Gary   It's gotta go back tomorrow.

Elaine (*off*)   Sorry?

Gary   *Saving Private Ryan!*

Elaine *re-enters with a bottle of perfume and her handbag.*

Elaine   Well we'll just have to save him another night won't we? Yer know I go out on Thursdays. It's karaoke night. The grand final's in a couple of weeks, yer should come, Gary. Could do with a bit of support. Might win a weekend to Skegness if I'm lucky.

Gary   No thanks.

Elaine   Oh come on, cheer up.

Elaine *sprays herself with the perfume.* **Gary** *sits at the table.*

Elaine   Why don't yer give Miles a ring?

Gary   Miles?

Elaine   I'm sure he'd love to watch . . . Whatsit called? Private who?

Gary   No. He'd probably just side with the Germans.

Elaine   You haven't seen 'im all week. He's over the moon with this new job of 'is.

Gary   When did you see 'im?

Elaine   He called.

Gary   When?

Elaine   Last night. Didn't I tell you? They're renovating one of the old houses down Scott Road. Should give 'im a ring.

Gary   No. Think I'll just get an early night.

Elaine   Well, suit yerself.

She grabs her coat from the back of the chair.

Gary   Yer not gonna be back late are yer?

Elaine   Depends if I make the quarter-finals or not.

She puts her handbag over her shoulder.

Now. 'Material Girl' or 'Thank You for the Music'?

Gary   What?

Elaine   Which one would you go for? 'Material Girl''s got a bit more bite hasn't it? But yer can't go wrong with Abba.

Gary   How should I know?

Elaine   Yer follow the charts don't yer?

Gary   Well . . . What did you do last week?

Elaine   'Thank You for the Music'.

Gary   Do the other one then.

Elaine   Yer don't think I'm a bit too old for Madonna?

Gary   Mum, please, I don't know. Just do whatever feels comfortable.

Elaine   Half of it's in the routine anyway. The showmanship. Bit of cleavage, few dancesteps. Should've seen the state of us at the disco the other night. Lottie and me. Woman doesn't know when to stop. Dozen G&T's and she's dancing on the table with 'er skirt above 'er 'ead. 'Get down,' I yell, 'yer'll get us all chucked out carryin' on like that.' Next thing yer know I'm up there with 'er. Me n'Kay and that young girl, Scampi. What's that bloody song now? You should know, it's a classic. One with all the car mechanics.

Gary   Who?

Elaine   In the video. 'Uptown Girl', that's it. Haven't danced like that in years. Not on a table anyway. Lucky I was only on the Smirnoffs. Poor little Scampi slipped on a beer mat and broke 'er ankle. Arse over tit in the middle o'the dancefloor. I told yer we had to carry 'er home dint I? Yeah, well. None o' that nonsense tonight. Gonna win that holiday, you see if I don't.

Gary   I put some lekky in the meter.

Elaine   Oh, yer a good boy.

She spies and picks up the letter off the table.

What is this? Is this the . . . ?

Gary *snatches the letter out of her hand.*

Gary   Mum!

Elaine   What is it?

Pause.

Gary?

Elaine *sits at the table.*

You all right, love? What is it, eh?

Gary   It's from the college. Down London?

Elaine *takes the letter from* **Gary***'s hand, she reads it. Long pause.*

Elaine   Gary! Why didn't you tell me? (*Reads.*) 'We are pleased to accept your application for the BA degree course in Television and Media Studies, commencing 6 September 2000. Details of the course and the site will be sent to you by . . .' You did it, son. You . . .

She hugs and kisses **Gary**.

. . . bloody well did it! Why didn't you tell me before? This is wonderful news! London! I knew yer'd do it, I knew it!

Gary   All right, all right.

Gary *takes the letter and stands.*

Just leave it, yeah?

Elaine   Leave it? Gary. Sit down, son.

Gary   Yer gonna be late.

Gary *exits.*

Scene Four

Pete's *bedroom. Night. Dim lights fade up.*

Pete *and* **Carol**, *naked in the bed.*

Long pause.

Carol   Are you all right?

Pause.

Pete *moves off* **Carol**, *lays on his back.*

Carol   Pete? . . . Pete, what's wrong?

Pause.

'Ave yer done already? I don't mind.

Pause.

Pete?

Pete   Look . . .

Pause.

D'yer mind if we turn the light off?

Carol   Is it somethin' I've done?

Pete   No, it's just . . . I feel more comfortable in the dark.
It's not you or nothin'.

Carol *turns the bedside lamp off.*

Carol   There. 'Ow's that?

Pete   Yeah.

Long pause.

Carol   Well, is that better or not? I'm not used to this
either, yer know?

Pete   Eh?

Carol   I don't just sleep with any old bloke.

Pete   Did I say that?

Carol   I know, it's just . . . I thought I'd done something
wrong.

Pete   No. 'Course not.

Carol   Never thought it'd be like this.

Long pause.

Pete   Maybe we should close our eyes n'all.

Carol   It's not 'cause I'm fat is it?

Pete   No.

Carol   Most blokes wunt look twice at me.

Pete   Don't care if yer fat or not. Dunt bother me, none
o'that. Never 'as.

Carol   That's why I wear black all the time. Try n'hide the
flab.

Pete   Were yer thinkin' about me?

Carol   Eh?

Pete   Just then. Were yer thinkin' 'bout me? In yer 'ead.

Carol   Yer know I was. 'Ant got no other choice 'ave I?
Wunt be 'ere otherwise.

Pete   Course yer gotta choice. That's what this is all about
init? You comin' 'ere. Try it.

Carol   Eh?

Pete   Close yer eyes. Go on.

Carol   We don't have to do this, Pete. Don't feel obliged.
Yer've done enough already. Wunt be in a bed at all if it
weren't for you. Could o'been sleepin' on streets or owt. We
don't have to do anythin' if yer don't want.

Pete   Look, just close yer eyes, all right?

Carol   But . . .

Pete   Fucksake, Carol.

Carol   There's no need to swear.

Pete   Just do it then. For me.

Carol   I knew this'd happen. Soon as we got into bed, I saw
the way you looked at me. Dint know whether to laugh or cry
did yer?

Pete   It's nothin' to do with you, all right?

Carol   Then what is it then? I can't help the way I look,
I've got a disorder. Do yer think I like lookin' like this?

Pete *straddles* **Carol**.

Pete   Look, I'm gonna stick it in yer, all right?

Carol   Pete . . .

Pete   Just gi'it a few seconds. Close yer eyes.

Pause.

Can yer feel it?

Carol Yeah.

Pete OK. Now just keep 'em shut.

Carol Right.

Pete Yer done it?

Carol Yeah.

Pete They shut?

Carol Yes.

Pete Right. Now, don't do anythin' stupid. Yer name's Elaine, right?

Carol Elaine?

Pete That's right.

Carol You are joking aren't yer? Elaine? Elaine who?

Pete Dunt matter who she is. That's point.

Carol Who's Elaine, Pete?

Pete Just trust me, all right? Close yer eyes.

Carol I don't like this.

Pete Yer not even tryin'.

Carol Can't we just talk?

Pete No.

Carol Please, Pete, yer scarin' me now.

Pete Look, just think of someone. Some bloke.

Carol Eh?

Pete Someone yer like, someone yer fancy.

Carol But . . .

Pete   Dunt even have to be real if yer don't want.

Carol   I'm with you aren't I?

Pete   No yer not. Pete dunt exist, all right? Forget about 'im.

Carol   This is stupid.

Pete   No it int. Go on. It's just a game int it? Think of someone.

Carol   Who?

Pete   I dunno, Mel Gibson, Brad Pitt. Who'd yer last 'ave a wank about?

Carol   Pete!

Pete   Yer don't have to tell me or owt. Just think about 'em.

Carol   Can't I just think of you?

Pete   No.

Carol   But . . .

Pete   I said no, Carol. Look, we either do this properly or we don't do it at all.

Carol   But, Pete, I can't just switch . . .

Pete   Trust me. It's magic.

Carol   I can't, it's stupid.

Pete   Yes yer can, go on, shut yer eyes. I'm not gonna hurt yer.

Long pause.

Well? Yer thought of someone?

Pause.

Elaine. Have you thought of someone?

Carol   I can't.

Pete   Just say somert . . .

Carol   What?

Pete   A name. Call me a name.

Pause.

Call me Donald.

Carol   Donald?

Pete   Yeah.

Carol   What, like Donald Duck?

Pete   If yer like.

Carol (*laughs*)   Donald.

Pete   Yeah.

Carol   Donald.

Pete   See? That's better already. Can yer feel it?

Pause.

I told yer it were magic dint I?

Pause.

Elaine. I told yer dint I?

Scene Five

Building site. Early morning. Half-built wall, cement mixer, pile of bricks. Radio playing.

Errol *is busy laying bricks.*

Miles *enters, in a hurry.*

Miles   Only gone and lumped me with a court summons 'ant they? Eight hundred bastard quid. No sorry, eight hundred and seventy-three bastard quid.

Errol   Eh?

Miles   Fuckin' council tax wankers! Take me forra prick!

Miles *quickly removes his coat. As they speak,* **Miles** *joins* **Errol** *in the brick-laying.* **Miles** *works ferociously and clumsily.*

Errol   You're jokin'.

Miles   I wish I wa'. Been on the fuckin' phone for over an hour tryin' to sort it out. I've only just signed off. But oh no, they don't 'ave any record of that do they? That's not on their fuckin' files. Suddenly I'm in debt eight hundred quid and they're playin' rinky-dinky-tink Mozart down me ear. 'Sorry, your call is in a queue. Please hold the line and we'll connect you to one of our customer service operators.' Customer service operators! More like brain-dead cunts, fuck yer life up operators! Honest, Errol, I've 'ad it up to 'ere, I've . . . I could fuckin' . . . Int the whole point of gettin' a job's so yer can clear yer debts? So yer can stay on top o'bills? 'Sorry, your call is in a queue.' Was better off on the dole. Stupid bitch couldn't even speak the language prop'ly. (*Bad Indian accent.*) 'No, Mr Frazer, there must be mistake some. Check file, no, nothing. Court in two week, yes' – I mean, where the fuck do they hire these people? Sounded like she'd just sailed up the bloody Ganges or somert – 'No, Mr Frazer, you contact legal aid yes.' Did you know, right? Did you know, they charge yer for like a year in advance?

Errol   Yeah. That's if yer can't make the monthly . . .

Miles   So, not only am I payin' for a debt that never existed – 'cause I was signin' on, all right? But I'm also payin' for twelve months that 'ant even 'appened yet. Might 'ave an 'eart attack tomorrow. What good'll it do me then, eh? And what are we payin' for anyway? I mean, fire brigade fair enough. But the cops?! What the fuck do they ever do that's worth eight 'undred quid? Sittin' on their fat arses all day, pullin' people up for non-payment of council tax when there's junkies n'rapists n'killers roamin' the streets scot free. Tell yer, we were better off with the Tories in power. Never 'ad

any o'this shite. Knew where yer were then. New fuckin'
Labour, call 'emselves Labour, bleedin' yer dry. Yuppie
bastard Blair grinnin' like a twat , sayin' 'e's out for the
people – fuck that. Who's he think we are, eh? Plebs, that's
what. Ignorant bloody plebs. Prick dunt know jack shit. Like
to see 'im sit in the social all day. 'Im and 'is brat in a
pushchair, givin' it all that mighty mouse bollocks in 'is Gucci
fuckin' haircut, yeah right. He'd shit 'imself. Too busy
nobbin' Cherie to give a fuck anyway. Snortin' coke off 'er
dirty flange every night. Yeah mate, they're all coke'eads, yer
know? Closet coke'ead faggots. It's Thatcher still runs this
country, not 'im. Wanker. Gotta go the dole office now. Get
another fuckin' form to prove that I'm not a fuckin' fraud,
sortin' out their mistakes. I said, I said to 'er, 'Can't you do
it?' 'No, Mr Frazer, you bring form to us.' Like, when 'ave I
got time to go the dole office? Eh? I'm a workin' man.

Errol I know.

Miles Sit in that shit-'ole all day because of them useless
bastards. Losin' money.

Miles and **Errol** *continue working.*

Long pause.

Errol Look, I know it's a pain in the arse, but . . .

Miles Yeah, I know, all right?

Errol Well, if yer do go down Legal Aid and talk to
someone there, yer can probably . . .

Miles I know, I know, it's not your problem.

Errol 'Ey, we're all in the same boat.

Miles Treat me like a kid, like I don't know what I'm
talkin' about.

Errol Look, just go down the Legal Aid, talk to them.
That's what they're there for, Miles. I know yer pissed off
n'that, but yer can't let it get yer down. They're not worth it,
mate.

Miles   Not somethin' yer really wanna wake up to, yer know?

Errol   Yeah, 'course.

Miles   Gonna have to break into me savin's at this rate.

Errol   Savin's?

Miles   Yeah, me dad left us some cash like. S'pposed to be an investment f'future.

Errol   I'd 'elp yer out mesen if I could.

Miles   Least I made it in time though, eh? Had to get a taxi from the flats. 'E dint say nothin' did 'e? Ron?

Errol   'Ant seen 'im meself yet.

Miles   Good. Don't want 'im thinkin' I'm a slack-arse, know what I mean? Only thing I've got goin' for me at moment. This place. Yer don't mind me doin' this bit do yer?

Errol   No. Go for it.

Miles   Sorry about all that . . . Yer know?

Errol   Honestly, Miles. Don't worry about it. Good to get it out yer system.

Miles   Go the sports centre at dinner. Try n'jog it off like.

Miles *lays bricks.* **Errol** *mixes cement.*

Long pause.

Errol   Who was that? Last night?

Miles   Eh?

Errol   In the pub last night. Sorry, it's not my business.

Miles   Pete. Me brother. You wunt know 'im. 'E were just a baby when we were kids. Still is now.

Errol   Nowt the matter is it? – Sorry. Tell me to shut up, I'm just . . .

Pause.

Yeah, well.

Errol *takes a break. Tea from a flask and a cigarette.*

Miles *keeps working.*

Long pause.

Errol Fuckin' does yer back in this dunt it?

Miles Could bloody murder 'im sometimes.

Errol Eh?

Miles Actin' like 'e's only one. Fuckin' cut me up n'all, yer know?

Errol What, yer brother?

Miles No, me dad, yer dick'ead.

Errol Oh. Right.

Miles Don't understand 'im. Just gotta try n'get on with it don't yer? 'Ard enough tryin' to get on with real world, never mind all that crap. Look at me, right? Twenny-eight years old. Can yer believe it? Feel like I only left school other day. What 'ave I got to show for it, eh?

Errol Wunt know, Miles.

Miles No. Yer not the only one either. Don't think no one bloody knows.

Long pause.

Errol Least yer got yer health though, eh? Miles?

Pause.

Can't be all bad. Still young after all. I mean . . .

Pause.

I mean I know yer've been through a lot o'shit, what with yer dad passin' away n'all this tax n'shit, n'everythin' . . . But, yer

know? That's how world works int it? Swings n'roundabouts.
I mean, we cunt 'ave spring without winter could we? Look at
me. I used to be like you. Dint think I'd ever turn mesen
round once the business fell through. Thought I were done
for. Might as well dig me own bloody grave and make meself
at 'ome. Pot o'fuckin' coffee on the headstone.

Pause.

I know how it feels, Miles. Yer not alone.

Long pause.

Ah, it'll be all right, yer'll see. Just try n'look on bright side.
'Ere.

He pulls some polaroids from his back pocket, moves over to **Miles**,
who has his back turned to him, working.

This might cheer you up. Look . . . Miles.

Miles *turns, his eyes are filled with tears.*

Errol   Miles . . .

Miles   What?!

Errol   Fuckin' 'ell.

Miles   Cheer me up?! Cheer me up?!

Errol   Look, forget about it, I . . .

Miles   No, come on!

He grabs the polaroids off **Errol**, *looks through them.*

Why not, eh?

Errol   Sorry, I shunt 'ave . . .

Miles   Arrr. Int that sweet. The little baby, look. Got your
eyes 'ant she?

Errol   Miles, please . . .

Miles   That the missis, yeah? Fuckin' landed on yer feet
there 'ant yer. Must be very proud.

He throws the polaroids across the yard.

Errol   All right, I'm sorry, there's no need to . . .
F'fucksake, Miles!

Miles (*crying*)   Give 'er one for me next time, eh? Give 'er a
good hard . . .

He leans back on the wall.

(*Crying.*)   . . . belt up the . . .

*The wall collapses, taking **Miles** with it.*

Scene Six

Pete's *bedroom. Morning.*

Carol *sitting on the edge of the bed, wrapped in the bed sheet. Her
rucksack in the corner of the room.*

Pete *lying on the bed, shuffling a pack of playing cards. They both
drink and smoke.*

Pause.

Carol   I left 'ome. Ran away. They'd gone on 'oliday to
Newquay. Left me to look after dog. Cunt bear it, barkin' n'
whinin' all through the night. Give me money to feed it, but it
never even et it. Tried every flavour in shop, Chum, Pal,
cheap stuff. By end o'first week, yer cunt see meat for flies.
Stank n'all. I mean, it were on its last legs anyway. Had it
since I were a kid. Bobby. As in Bobby Moore n'that. Spaniel.
Cunt walk properly, never mind run. Just lyin' in its basket all
day, wunt shut up. Woke me up in middle o'night cryin'.
Went downstairs to kitchen n'e's sprawled out by back door,
shakin'. Tongue's hangin' out, n'e's spittin' all this foam.
Cunt take me eyes off 'im. Just stood there, in dark, seemed
like hours. Pulled 'im up by scruff of 'is neck n'took 'im
upstairs to bath. Filled it up with hot water. Weighed a ton.
Got soaked when I threw 'im in. Just sank to bottom, like 'e
were made o' stone. Dint seem real.

Long pause.

I knew what they'd say. Should o'called vet. Stupid girl.

Pause.

Dunt feel like I'm there most o'time anyway. That'll fuckin' teach 'em.

Pete   Can stay 'ere. If yer want.

Carol   Dint want to go anyway. I 'ate 'olidays. I 'ate them.

Pete   Feels like yer gonna burst open any second dunt it?

Carol   Yeah. Don't care though. They can rot for all I care. Treat me like a kid. All me life. Thought about jumpin' in river once. River Don.

Pause.

I can't 'elp the way I look.

Pete   I sometimes think about dyin' n'all.

Carol   Yeah? Really?

Pete   All the time. Makes everythin' seem clearer some'ow.

Carol   I know. Sometimes think about catchin' cancer or AIDS or somert. Be great. That'd wake 'em up. Can imagine them both at me funeral, cryin' their fuckin' hearts out. Then they'd see what it's like. I've got me songs worked out n'everythin'. 'Wonderwall', 'Try' and 'When You Say Nothin' at All'. Gonna 'ave all me old school mates, Becky and Joanna, do a speech on my be'alf. Tell 'em what it were really like, me parents. Then they'll see. Make 'em tek us serious for once. Show 'em I meant it. Fuckin' hate this place. Look in the mirror and I wanna puke. Like to puke all over them. They don't do nothin', just sit there every night. Not even talkin'. Watchin' telly like a pair o'bloody zombies. Don't even love each other, never mind me. Fuckin' hit me across the face once. Been waggin' school n'that. Told 'er then I'd do it. Wanted me to go college and do retakes. Like that's gonna help. Stupid bitch.

Pause.

I'm never goin' back. Threw me keys down the drain n'everythin'.

Pete *moves to* **Carol**, *sits behind her, fingers her face with the tips of his fingers.*

Long pause.

Pete   Yer don't mind do yer? Not bein' funny or owt.

Carol   No.

Pete   Can 'elp yer, yer know? 'Elp each other.

Carol   Yeah? Dint know whether I should've come at all. Thought yer were gonna take me to police.

Pete   'Ant got long meself. Next few days. Be like magic. Two of us.

Pete *kisses* **Carol***'s head.*

Carol *kisses* **Pete***'s fingers.*

Pause.

Carol   We gonna be together then? From now on.

Pete   'Ant got nob'dy else.

Scene Seven

Elaine*'s flat. The kitchen. Day.*

Miles *sitting at the kitchen table.*

Gary *making tea.*

Gary   Yer shouldn't get yerself too worked up about it, Miles.

Miles   Sickenin' it is. Sickenin'.

Gary   There's other jobs out there, yer know? So it dint work out this time, so what?

Miles   I'll show 'im who's incompetent when I shove me 'ard 'at up 'is arse.

Gary   Yer dint knock the whole house down did yer?

Miles   No, just the wall. One crappy fuckin' wall.

Gary (*laughs*)   I'm sorry, it's just . . .

Miles   Yeah, go on, laugh.

Gary (*laughing*)   The thought of it . . .

Miles   Charlie bleedin' Chaplin, that's me.

Gary *finishes making the tea, sits at the table.*

Miles   Needed that job n'all. What with all this council tax shit. Not to mention the rent and the . . .

Gary   Phone bill and the lekky and the gas and the . . .

Miles   Water rates f'fucksake.

Gary   Way of the world, Miles.

Miles   Yeah, that's easy for you to say.

Gary   'Ey, I've done my time. I 'ad five years of the shit, remember?

Pause.

Miles   Bang goes the in'eritance.

Gary   Won't come to that will it?

Gary *lights a cigarette, and gives* **Miles** *one.*

Miles   Worst thing is, I get laid off n'that little prick dunt get shit. Not even a warnin'.

Gary   Who?

Miles   That black guy, Errol. Used to live down whatsit when we were kids? Fuckin' Eddy Grant reject, you know 'im. Built like a toothpick. Could snap 'im in two wi'me japs eye 'e's so small.

Gary   What's 'e got to do with it?

Miles   Fucker pushed me init?

Gary   Eh?

Miles   Yer don't just fall into walls for the fun of it, Gary. 'E was tryin' it on n'that. Givin' it all that . . . Ice T bollocks. 'Im n'is fuckin' baby.

Gary   But I thought yer said it were an accident.

Miles   Accident? The guy's been tryin' it on since we first started. Like 'e fuckin' knows me.

Gary   Did yer not tell the foreman?

Miles   Dint wanna know.

Gary   What, and no one saw?

Miles   All happened in a flash like. First thing I know he's gi'in' me all this shit – 'bout bein' white n'that – next thing I'm lyin' in a pile o'fuckin' bricks.

Gary   Should tell the manager, mate. The what-they-called? Tell the agency.

Miles   Ah, what's point?

Gary   Unfair fuckin' dismissal. Harassment.

Miles   Won't make any difference, Gary. Blacks don't get blamed for shit these days. Everyone's too fuckin' para 'bout startin' a riot.

Gary   Eh? This int about colour though.

Miles   Course it is. 'E's black and I'm white, end of fuckin' story.

Gary   You're full o'shit.

Miles   Me? Look around, yer blind bastard. 'Ave yer 'ad a walk round this area lately? 'Ow many white people d'yer see sittin' on the square down Spital Hill of an afternoon? 'Ow many white people d'yer see at all for that matter?

Gary   Yeah, but this is a mixed area, Miles. It 'as been for years. What about all the Asians n'Indians n'that?

Miles   That's what I'm talkin' about. Black.

Gary   Oh, fuck off.

Miles   They're all the same, Gary.

Gary   Bollocks.

Miles   And the blacker you are, the better you are. I see 'em all at night, Gary. All down past the precinct, from top o'Burngreave down into town. Lines of 'em, 'angin' outside shops in their fuckin' beemers. Or just stood there on corners, like packs of 'ounds, givin' it all that fuckin' Boyz n'the Hood bollocks. It's scary, mate. Don't know if I'm gonna get mugged, knifed, fuckin' shot. It's just a bloody game to them. Cunts don't know who they are no more, so they pretend to be fuckin' gangsters and that makes everythin' all right. They've even got them Blues init? Crack'ouses underneath shops, yer can 'ear 'em at night, playin' all that fuckin' ragga shite, keepin' the whole neighbourhood awake. But does anyone complain? No, let 'em 'ave their fun, they deserve it. This is their country now remember? Wankers. They're all bloody junkies anyway. Psychos, mate. I mean, if I'm scared, God knows what little old women who've lived 'ere all their lives, through the war n'that. They must be fuckin' petrified and that's what pisses me off. Good honest people who've struggled all their lives, who can't even go n'get their pension 'cause of all them cunts, intimidatin' 'em twenny-four seven and turnin' the area into a fuckin' drug den. They don't deserve that do they? Well?

Gary   Well what?

Miles   Do they deserve it?

Pause.

See? They've got you n'all. In yer own fuckin' home.

Gary   No, I'm just fed up with you goin' on about it, all right?

Miles   They take our jobs, our women, the whole bloody community. 'Alf of 'em can't even admit they're British and they were born 'ere. Hypocrites. Whingin' about Stephen fuckin' Lawrence every time yer turn on the telly, when they don't even wanna be 'ere in the first place. And we just sit 'ere like cunts, tekkin' it 'cause . . . 'Cause . . . .

Gary   Have yer quite done now?

Miles   'Cause o' slavery or somert.

Long pause.

Gary   D'yer want another brew? Mine's gone cold.

Pause.

Miles . . .

Miles   Be even worse down London yer know.

Gary   Yeah, well . . . Just 'ave to find out for mesen won't I?

*Enter **Elaine**, with shopping bags.*

Elaine   Oh. Well this is a nice surprise.

*She kisses **Miles** on the head.*

How are you, sausage?

Gary   'Ere.

Gary *takes the shopping bags off **Elaine**. He puts them on the side and proceeds to unload the food.*

Elaine   Well? How's the new job?

Miles   Yeah. It's really good actually, Mum. Just finished now. Knackered.

Elaine (*laughs, pinches his cheek*)   Arrr. Look at his little face.
Put 'im to bed with a cocoa.

Miles   Mum.

Elaine   No, honestly, I'm really pleased for yer, Miles.
About time yer started gettin' back on yer feet.

Miles   Thanks.

Elaine   I suppose Gary told you his good news as well?

Miles   Yeah.

Elaine   Mmm. Proper little Dick Whittington, eh?

Miles   Yeah, that's great.

Elaine   But without the cat of course. Well, come on.

Miles   What?

Elaine *takes her coat off.*

Elaine   Tell me all about it then, Miles.

Miles   There's not really much to tell, Mum. Just cheap
labour, yer know?

Elaine *goes to help* **Gary** *with the bags.*

Gary   Oh no, that's all right, sit down.

Elaine   But . . .

Gary   Mum.

Long pause.

Elaine *sits at the table.*

Elaine   Well I would offer to make you some dinner . . .

Miles   No, I'm fine, honest.

Elaine   . . . If I hadn't already made plans.

Pause.

I'm going on a date.

Miles *and* **Gary**   What?

Miles   You're kiddin'. Mum!

Gary   Who is 'e?

Elaine   No one you know. 'E was at the Catherine Arms the other night. Karaoke night. He's taking me out to dinner.

Gary   Who is 'e?

Elaine   Well, he's forty-five, tall . . . Very charming.

Miles   What's his name?

Elaine   Beautiful complexion.

Miles   Mum.

Elaine   Well . . . His real name's Clement. But he likes to be called – wait for it. Horse.

Miles *and* **Gary**   Horse?!

Elaine (*laughs*)   I know, it's hysterical isn't it? . . . Very sweet with it though. He comes from Jamaica.

Pause.

What?

Scene Eight

Pete'*s bedroom. Day. A week later. Music playing from the stereo.*

On the bed is a shoebox full of photographs. Some of them are scattered on the sheets. **Carol** *sits on the bed, a small mirror balanced on her legs. She applies makeup and pulls faces at her reflection.*

Pete *enters the room, unseen by* **Carol***. He carries two plastic bags full of shopping. He stands in the entrance of the room, watching* **Carol***.*

Long pause.

Pete   Thought we'd go forra drive later.

Carol *jumps, dropping the mirror.*

Carol   Pete!

She gets off the bed, moves to **Pete**.

I've been worried sick.

She hugs **Pete**, *kisses him.*

Thought yer'd forgotten about me. Fled the country or
somert.

Pete   'Ere.

He takes a packet of cigars out of the shopping bag and gives them to
Carol.

Pete   They'd run out o'Bensons.

Carol   Oh . . .

Pete   Don't mind d'yer?

Carol   I don't mind.

Pete   Good.

Carol   Where've yer been?

Pete *puts the shopping down on the bed.*

Pause.

Pete *sees the scattered photographs on the bed, and picks one up.*

Carol   Yeah, I . . . I were tidyin' up before. Found 'em
under the bed there. Sorry. Cunt 'elp meself.

Pause.

That's yer dad int it? Thought so. Spittin' image o'you.
Thought it was you forra second. Big sad eyes n'that. Yer
don't mind d'yer? Been over a week now, Pete. You n'me.

Pete *rips up the photo.*

Carol   I like this one. On the beach n'that.

She grabs one of the photographs and shows it to **Pete***.*

'Ard to imagine yer parents when they were young. Looks like another world dunt it? Out of a film or somert.

Pause.

Must've really loved each other though. There's lipstick on 'is cheek, look.

She kisses **Pete** *on the cheek.*

Pause.

I 'ant been t'the beach in yonks. Is that you in the pushchair?

Pause.

Pete? You all right?

Pete *grabs* **Carol** *and kisses her.*

Long pause.

Carol   D'yer think we'll ever have kids? I wunt mind if we dint.

Pete   There's some vodka if yer want.

He empties the bags on to the bed. Bottles, cans, ice cream, crisps, etc.

I put some petrol in car. Thought we'd go forra drive later.

He takes one of the plastic bags and begins stuffing the photographs inside it.

After all. That's what we agreed.

Carol *grabs the mirror off the bed, moves aside. Her back to* **Pete***,* **Carol** *reapplies her makeup.*

Pete   'E wunt've sent yer otherwise. 'Ad to 'appen sooner or later. 'E told me yer'd come. Can't turn back now. 'E'll be waitin'.

Carol *turns back to* **Pete***.*

Carol   Well? What d'yer think?

Pause.

Pete?

She moves to the bed and sits on the edge, opposite **Pete**.

Me mum'd kill us lookin' like this.

The photos are stuffed in the plastic bag. **Pete** *ties the handles together.*

Carol   I left a message on the answerin' machine. While you were out. Told 'em I'm serious this time. I mean . . . I'm not in the way am I? Yer don't mind?

Pete   No. Somert yer'd rather be doin'?

Carol   'Course not.

Pete   Well then. Me neither. That's why it's gonna work.

Pause.

Carol   I've never met anyone like you before.

She touches **Pete**.

Come to bed. I'll call yer Donald again if yer like. I don't mind. Donald.

Pete *picks up the bottle of vodka, opens it and takes a swig.*

Pete   Thought we'd go forra drive later. Be good for us.

He offers the bottle to **Carol**.

Go on. Take it.

Carol *hesitates, takes the bottle.*

Pete   Stops damp gettin' in yer 'ead.

Carol   Damp?

Pete   Yeah. We do wanna do this prop'ly don't we? Spent last o'me wages on this little lot, can't let it go to waste. Go on. Carol. Go on.

Carol   I am!

She swigs the vodka and splutters.

Carol   Uuuurgh.

Pete *laughs.*

Carol   Don't laugh!

She drinks.

Pete *takes the plastic bag and moves to the door.*

Carol   Pete? Where yer goin'?

Pete   I'll only be a minute. Bin men come tomorrow.

Carol   But yer've only . . .

Pete   Just sit tight will yer? And don't look at me like that.

Carol   Yer do still love me don't yer?

Pete   'Course. You know I do. Got it all worked out 'ant I?

Scene Nine

Running track, sports centre. Day.

Miles *jogging round the sports track, in shorts, listening to a walkman.*

Miles (*to himself*)   And 'ere 'e comes, one more lap to go. Miles Frazer and Linford Christie, neck n'neck. Two giants of the sportin' world . . . Christie takes the corner, but what's this? Frazer takes Christie by storm. And it's Frazer in the lead . . . Mad Dog Miles Frazer!

Errol (*off*)   Miles!

Miles   And the crowd are goin' wild!

Enter **Errol**, *in his work gear, hard hat in hand.*

Errol   Miles, thankfuck.

Miles *runs past* **Errol**.

Errol   Miles!

Miles   Headin' toward the finishin' line . . .

Errol   Miles, mate!

He chases after **Miles**.

'Old up!

Miles   Takes the final corner, but . . .

Errol   Miles!

He runs after **Miles**, *catches up with him.*

Miles   . . . can he do it? Another gold medal for the prince of Pitsmoor and . . .

Errol (*grabs* **Miles**)   Jesus Christ, Miles.

Miles (*jumps*)   F'fucksake!

Errol   Sorry, I . . .

Miles   The fuck yer doin'?! Frightened the life outta me, yer prick.

Miles *turns his walkman off.*

Errol   I've been lookin' for yer everywhere.

Miles   Can't yer see I'm busy?

Errol   Dint know where else to turn.

Pause.

Miles *catches his breath.*

Errol   Honestly, Miles, I've been goin' spare.

Miles   Yer've got a bloody nerve 'ant yer?

Errol   I said I'm sorry dint I?

Miles   Showin' yer face after last week. Lucky I don't give you a slap.

Errol   Eh?

Miles (*slaps chest*)   See this? Like char-grilled sirloin, mate. Could break a chair over these tits and I'd still be standin'.

Errol   What yer talkin' about?

Miles   Just don't be messin' all right?

Errol   I'm not!

Miles   D'yer realise 'ow much that's cost me? I needed that fuckin' job.

Errol   Yeah?

Miles   Yeah. Exactly.

Errol   I know.

Miles   Well then. Think I deserve an apology don't you?

Errol   Eh? What did I do?

Miles   What . . . ? Yer fuckin' provoked me init?

Errol   The wall collapsed!

Miles   No thanks to you.

Errol   It were an accident weren't it?

Miles   If you'd been doin' yer job like yer shoulda done . . .

Errol   Oh, come on, Miles, don't be like that.

Miles   I wunt be in this fuckin' mess! Back on the dole. No one'll employ me no more. Bastards tried sendin' me to Burger King the other day. 'Ad to tell 'em I was a vegetarian, like I'm some sort of trippy hippy incense-burnin' gobshite.

Errol   All right, I . . .

Miles   And the Council Tax still won't listen. Got the bailiffs on me case now. Now I'm not workin' no more. 'Ad to go back social other day, right? Wankers've lost the forms from the week before. I still don't exist.

Errol   Look, I'm sorry, all right? I did try.

Miles   Try?

Errol   Yeah, I spoke to Ron. The foreman? I told 'im it were an accident. I said there were a problem with the cement mixer, that's why it went down like that. Honest, Miles, it's not like I don't care. Yer know what 'e's like. Man's a power freak.

Miles   Gonna 'ave to use all me savin's now.

Errol   No yer don't.

Miles   Me dad's money, sponked on fuckin' taxes that I shunt 'ave to pay for in first place.

Errol   Miles, listen. I can help yer, all right?

Miles   Don't yer think yer've done enough damage already?

Errol   Why d'yer think I'm 'ere? I've been all over town lookin' for you. I need a favour.

Miles   Favour my cock.

Errol   I'll pay yer for it like.

Miles   'Ow much?

Errol   Yer don't even know what it is yet.

Miles   It's not illegal is it?

Errol   Eh?

Miles   I'm not messin' with no drugs or owt.

Errol   Who said owt about drugs?

Miles   I know what your . . .

Pause.

Errol   What? I need a babysitter, yer daft sod. That's all. Smack. I'm a married man.

Miles   Sorry. I forgot. Babysittin', yer say?

Errol   Yeah, for tonight like. Somert came up. Family thing. Dint know who else to ask. Usually get me sister to do it, but she's got one o'them salsa classes tonight. Dint know who else to ask.

Miles   Dunt involve changin' nappies does it?

Errol   Bloody 'ell, it's not that complex. She'll be asleep by seven anyway. Yer can watch telly all night if yer want. Rent a video out. I'll even lay a bit o'food on for yer. Few beers. It's only till I get back. Won't be any later than twelve. Come on, Miles, yer said yer needed the money. Call it thirty. Thirty quid, and, say, a fiver's worth o'cans.

Miles   Forty.

Errol   Forty then.

Miles   I'm not singin' no lullabies or owt.

Errol   Look, d'yer want the job or not? Be doin' each other a favour won't we? I'm only askin' 'cause I trust yer. We're mates aren't we? 'Ere.

He pulls out his wallet.

Forty quid, yeah?

Pause.

Well, come on, make yer mind up, I'm gonna be late.

Miles   All right then. Yeah.

Errol   Oh, that's fuckin' . . .

*He shakes **Miles**'s hand, gives him money.*

Errol   . . . great, Miles. Yer a life saver.

Scene Ten

Car – moving. Day.

Pete *is driving,* **Carol** *is sitting in the passenger seat.* **Carol** *eats from a tub of ice cream.*

Music playing loudly – the Stone Roses' 'Begging You'.

Carol (*shouting*)   Pete! . . . Pete! Where we goin'?! . . . Pete!

Pete   What?!

Carol *turns the car stereo down.*

Carol   I said, where we goin'? You 'ant said nothin' since we left the flat.

Pete *accelerates.*

Carol   Pete.

Pete   It's a surprise, all right? Pass us one o'them cans.

Carol *takes a can of lager from the cans and gives it to* **Pete**. *He opens it and drinks.*

Carol   That's dangerous that. Yer shunt do that, Pete. Where we goin'?

Pete   Just shut it will yer?

Carol   You aren't well are yer? Yer don't look right.

Pete   I'm fine.

Carol   Yer shakin', Pete.

Pause.

Don't know where we goin' at all do yer?

Pause.

Pete! Let's not fight. Can't 'elp each other if yer won't talk to me.

Pete   I told yer, it's a surprise.

Pause.

Carol   Best not be lyin'.

Pete *drinks / drives,* **Carol** *eats.*

Carol *(with a mouthful of ice cream)*   Look! We're comin' up to
Chesterfield, look! Yer can see the spire on the . . .

Pete *turns up the music on the car stereo, drowning out* **Carol**. *He
accelerates.*

Scene Eleven

Phonebox fixed to a wall on the street behind **Elaine**'*s flat.*

Night. Raining.

Gary *in the phonebox, clutching a handful of change. He holds the
receiver to his ear. As he speaks, he intermittently puts money into the
box.*

Gary   Hello? . . . Hello, is Sophie there please? . . . It's Gary
. . . Yeah, how are you? . . . Not bad, same as always really
. . . I know, it 'as 'ant it? Over a year . . . Nothin' really, yer
know? . . . Is she there? . . . Oh no, if it's inconvenient, I'll . . .
All right . . . Yeah, yeah, good to speak to you too . . .
Thanks.

Pause.

Receiver to his ear, **Gary** *fumbles through his change and puts more
coins in the box.*

Gary   Hello? Sophie? . . . Yeah, I'm just, yer know? . . .
Thought I'd say hello, let yer know I'm still alive . . . Yeah . . .
How's it . . . Do I? . . . No, I think I've just gotta bit of a cold
. . . You sound the same . . . I said, you . . . Where? . . .
Ireland? . . . What? . . . No, I've never heard of them . . . *The
Tempest* – what, is that a play? . . . Yeah, I know it is, I'm . . .
Oh, right . . . And that's schools, yeah? . . . Really? Six
months . . . Yeah . . . Well, you always said that agent was a

bit of a . . . Yeah . . . Never knew how to cast you did they?
. . . Oh, that's really good . . . Mm . . . So yer gonna 'ave yer
name up in lights now? . . . Right . . . Be able to sample some
of the local Guinness though . . . Yeah . . . Good for the
circulation . . . When yer goin'? . . . This Friday? . . . Fuckin'
hell . . . Yeah . . . 'Course . . . Me? . . . Oh, yer know? Same
old same old . . . No, I'm workin' down some building site
down . . . Yeah . . . Down town, I know . . . With Miles n'that
. . . Yeah . . . Oh yeah, he 'ant changed . . . Thinkin' of . . .
Yeah . . . Yeah, I will do . . . You know me . . . 'Course! . . .
'Ey, I went down Rivelin the other day, on the bike n'that.
Saw that old man again . . . With 'is homemade rod, yeah . . .
made out of bamboo, Oriental style. Cunt believe it . . . No,
me neither. Still 'ant caught nothin' . . . 'E remembered you
. . . 'Where's that pretty young lass with the feathers in 'er
'at?' . . . Told 'im you were back at home, stuffin' pillows . . .
Well, I cunt could I? . . . Yeah, I know we're not, but . . .
What? . . . Who? . . . Who's Michael? . . . No . . . No, yer
never . . . He's a what? . . . A driving instructor? . . . Oh, right
. . . Is he gonna go and see you in Ireland? . . . Oh . . . Well,
that'll be nice won't it? . . . What? . . . Oh, yer know. Nothin'
serious anyway . . . Too busy for owt like that anyway. . .
Listen, d'yer fancy meetin' up? . . . Before yer go away
like? . . . Just a drink or somert . . . It'd be great t'see yer . . .
Oh . . . Right . . . Well, maybe for just an hour or somert,
if . . . Yeah? . . .

He checks his change, he has run out of silver.

Over the following, **Elaine** *enters, dressed for a night out, holding a
half-eaten kebab. She is very drunk.*

Gary   Oh, fuck it . . . No, it's just . . . I'm in a phonebox . . .
Look, yer couldn't ring me back could yer? . . . Yeah it's –
Shit, there's the pips, have yer got a pen? . . . Right, it's 0
double one . . .

The phone is cut off.

Fuck!

He anxiously rummages through his pockets for change.

Fucksake.

Elaine *collapses into the wall by the phonebox and retches.*

Gary *jumps back, dropping the receiver.*

Gary   Jesus Christ.

Elaine   Oh God, oh . . .

Elaine *nearly heaves again.*

Gary   Mum?

He quickly moves to **Elaine***'s side and grabs her.*

Mum! F'Godssakes, what . . . ?

Elaine, *groaning, held by* **Gary**, *pulls herself up.*

Elaine   Never again, never again.

Gary   What's happened?!

Elaine   Oh, Gary, thank God you're . . .

Gary   You've been attacked haven't you?! I knew it! I fuckin' knew it!

Elaine   Where am I?

Gary   Oh Christ . . .

Elaine   My head, ohhh.

Gary   Look, it's gonna be OK, all right? What happened? Who was it?

Elaine   Tequila.

Gary   What?

Elaine   Bloody tequila. In the pub . . .

Gary (*realises*)   Oh God.

Elaine   One pound fifty a shot. Slammers.

Gary   Come on.

He escorts **Elaine** *down the street.*

Elaine   I didn't think . . . Started spinnin'.

Scene Twelve

Car parked in the countryside. Night. The headlights still shining.

Carol *in the passenger seat.*

Pete *standing outside, smoking a cigarette, bottle in hand.*

Long pause.

Carol   Why 'ave we stopped?

Pause.

Where are we?

Pause.

Startin' to piss me off now.

Long pause.

I said yer startin' to piss me off, Pete!

Pete   This is it.

Carol   What?

Pete   We're 'ere.

Carol   Here? Here where? We're in the middle of fuckin' nowhere!

Pete   Get out.

Carol   But . . .

Pete   Just do it.

Carol   I can't see a thing. I'm scared, Pete. I'm scared n'I'm cold and . . . Place stinks o'shit n'all.

Pause.

Please, Pete, let's be friends, I don't wanna . . .

Pete   I said get out!

Carol   Pete . . .

Pete   Now!! This was your idea too, remember?

He exits into the darkness.

(Off.) Come on!

Pause.

Carol *hesitates.*

Pete *(off)*   Carol! We're nearly there now, come on!

Pause.

Carol *peers through the window.*

Carol   Pete? Where are yer? Don't leave me 'ere, Pete!

Pause.

Carol *lights a cigarette.*

Pause.

A cow moos, off.

Pete!!

Scene Thirteen

Errol's *lounge. Night. Television is on, connected to a playstation.*
Miles's *bag by the coffee-table. Can of beer and leftover takeaway on
coffee-table.*

Miles *is sitting on the sofa, playing the playstation – a 'track and field'
game.*

Miles *(to the screen, tapping the joypad in a frenzy)*   Come on yer
bastard, run! . . . Fuckin' . . . That's it, come on, come on . . .

I'm pressin' triangle, yer prick, jump! . . . And another! . . .
Yes, that's it, come on . . . Come on, fuckin' . . .

Sound of a baby crying, offstage.

Shit! (*Calls to the baby.*) It's all right, baba, daddy's goin' . . .
(*To the game.*) Bollocks! Get up yer . . . ! Jammy bastard yanks
every bloody . . . !

He tries to continue playing the game.

The baby's cries get louder and louder.

Jesus!

He stands, throws the joystick down.

Seven o'clock my arse!

He exits into the backroom.

(*Off.*) It's all right, sweetheart, Milesy's 'ere, look . . . Milesy
Smilesy, yes . . . Don't cry . . . Milesy doesn't like it when you
cry . . . Can't play playstation if you cry, can I? . . . Drives me
up the wall dunt it, yes? . . . Come on, sweet'eart, don't cry,
don't . . .

Pause.

(*Off.*) Look, just shut it will yer?! How d'you like it?! (*Mimics the
baby.*) Ooowaaaaah! Waaaaah! All bloody night!

The baby stops crying, starts giggling.

(*Off.*) Oh, yeah, that's hysterical init? I try to be kind, I try to
be reasonable, I try to . . .

Pause.

(*Off.*) What's that . . . ? . . . Have you just . . . ?

Pause.

(*Off.*) Oh, fuckin' . . . !

*He re-enters, slamming the door behind him, clutching his face, almost
retching.*

Fuckin' 'ell fire! Ohh. How do you do that? Arrr, Jesus H . . .

The baby's giggling subsides.

Miles *composes himself.*

Pause.

Right, that's it.

He rushes to his bag and starts packing his playstation away.

Forty quid or no forty quid, I'm not takin' . . . this shit, bloody scam.

He grabs the bag, then grabs his jacket off the sofa, makes to go.

Take me forra prick . . .

He spots a wooden African head on the side.

Pause.

He picks it up, investigates it.

Long pause.

He slips it in his bag.

Pause.

He looks round the room. He spots a dozen more ethnic ornaments. He hesitates.

Pause.

He moves round the room, filling his bag with the ornaments.

Miles   Fuck it.

Pause.

He moves to the video recorder. He hesitates.

Pause.

He drops his bag, moves to the video recorder, and begins disconnecting it.

Miles   All the same anyway. Probably dunt even know 'ow it works.

He has disconnected the video recorder and picks it up.

'Im n' 'is fuckin' salsa . . .

The door is heard opening, offstage.

He drops the video.

(*Whispered*.) Shit!

He frantically grabs the bag, and starts replacing the ornaments.

Fuckin', fuckin', fuckin' . . .

He drops the wooden African head on the floor.

(*Whispered*.)   Fuckin' shit it!

He picks it up; it has broken into two pieces.

Fuckin' shit it, fuckin' . . .

Enter **Errol**.

Miles *hides the African head behind his back.*

Miles   Oh, all right there, Errol. Dint 'ear yer come in.

Errol *says nothing, sits on the sofa.*

Long pause.

Errol   Got any beer left?

Miles *quickly puts the African head in his bag.*

Miles   What's that?

Errol *picks up the can of beer from the table and starts swigging it.*

Miles   Oh, yeah. That's all right. I'd finished wi'it anyway.

Errol *takes a remote control off the table, points it at the stereo, and presses a button. Music comes on, an R&B ballad.*

Errol *continues to drink, lights a cigarette.*

Long pause.

Miles   Er . . . Baby's all right. Quiet as a mouse all night.

Errol *shuts his eyes.*

Pause.

Miles   Yeah, well. I'll be off then.

He grabs his bag and coat, makes for the door.

I mean, if yer ever need me to do it again, I'll be more than . . .

Errol *starts crying.*

Pause.

Miles   Errol?

Errol *opens eyes, crying into his hands.*

Miles *starts edging out the door.*

Miles   Tell yer what, yer've got me number 'ant yer? We'll go out forra drink sometime.

Pause.

'Ey, take it easy, yeah?

Errol (*still crying*)   Miles?

Miles   Sorry, mate, it's already gone half twelve, I've got to . . .

Errol   Miles, please! Don't . . .

Pause.

Don't leave me. Not tonight.

Long pause.

Miles   Somert wrong?

Pause.

Errol.

Pause.

Fucksake, Errol, just . . .

Errol   I'm fallin' apart 'ere!

Miles   Eh?

Errol   I don't know what t' fuckin' do!

Pause.

I don't . . .

Miles   D'yer want another beer?

Errol   Me life.

Miles   Eh?

Errol   I want me life back.

Miles   Errol, mate, come on. Yer worse than the bloody baby.

Errol   Can't 'elp it, I . . . Can't take this, I can't . . .

Miles   'Ere, fuckin' get a grip will yer?

*He takes a four-pack of beer from his bag and joins **Errol** on the sofa.*

Get a grip, mate, come on. Can't be bad as all that surely.

*He opens two of the cans of beer and gives one to **Errol**.*

Pause.

Errol   Thanks.

Errol *drinks, still crying.*

Miles   That's better now int it, eh?

Pause.

There's still some korma if yer want it.

Errol   No. Thanks, I . . .

Pause.

Oh God.

Miles (*grabs the remote*)   'Ere, well, yer can turn that down forra fuckin' start. Yer'll 'ave me cryin' in a minute.

He turns the music down.

Now are yer gonna tell me what's up?

Pause.

F'fucksake, Errol, I can't . . .

Errol   It's Claire.

Miles   Who?

Errol   Me wife.

Miles   Yeah, and? 'Ere, she's not run off wi'some greasy old Spaniard 'as she?

Long pause.

She 'ant.

Errol   I was s'pposed to be pickin' 'er up from the station tonight. I thought there was somethin' wrong when she phoned last night. Never this though. Wasn't meant to 'appen like that.

Miles   Yer've seen 'er then?

Errol   Yeah. Both of 'em. Standin' there like . . . Like Tom n'fuckin' Nicole, hands in each others pockets. They're stayin' down the Victoria Hotel. Probably shaftin' 'er one as we speak. Big Spanish cock slooshin' 'er out in 'is fake Mediterranean shirt, I'll kill 'im, I'll fuckin' . . .

Miles   Errol!

Errol   Rip 'is fuckin' bollocks off!

Miles   Look, let's just take it easy, yeah? Deep breaths, all right.

Errol   Bastard shook my 'and. The nerve! Standin' there, grinnin' at me, like I'm s'pposed to just tek it! 'Yeah, that's right, mate, piece o'fuckin' piss. Six years down the drain, but

hey. Who am I to complain?' Go on, knife me in the heart, I
don't care! Knife me in the fuckin' heart, you bitch! Cunt!
Fuckin' slut!

Miles   Calm down, all right?

Errol *kicks over the coffee-table.*

Miles   Errol!

Errol *throws his beer across the room.*

Miles   Look, yer gonna wake the baby if yer carry on like
that.

Errol   I love 'er, Miles. She's all . . . She's all I've ever had,
I can't . . .

Miles   'Ey. It's all right, mate. Errol.

Pause.

Come on, Errol. Don't be like this.

Errol   I thought, I thought . . . Me n'er. S'pposed to be the
one, yer know?

Miles   I know.

Errol *holds out his finger, shows his wedding ring.*

Errol   And now look at it. Wasted.

Miles   Don't be daft. Errol. Look at me, Errol. Remember
what yer said? Don't cry. Come on, mate, yer better than
this, yer better than her. I mean . . . Swings n'roundabouts,
yeah?

Errol   They're goin' back on Tuesday. She's comin' round
tomorrow to pick up 'er things. I knew there was somethin'
wrong. When she phoned, I . . . I could 'ear it in 'er voice.
Should've known. Should've fuckin' known.

Miles   She's not tekkin' the kid is she?

Errol   We've got a meetin' tomorrow. In that pub on
Division Street. Yates's Wine Lodge. Discuss terms.

Miles   Yeah, but . . .

Errol   Over my fuckin' dead body.

Miles   Shit, Errol, I . . .

Pause.

I don't know what to say.

Errol   Guess it were bound to 'appen sooner or later. Ever since the business fell apart. Me brother shootin' all the money up 'is arms.

Miles   Eh?

Errol   'E were a junkie, Miles.

Miles   Oh . . .

Errol   Fuckin' skag'ead. Don't even know where 'e is no more. Could be dead for all I know. Stupid bastard did a runner once the money dried out.

Miles   Jesus Christ.

Errol   Fuckin' killed us too. Killed me, killed Claire . . . Everythin' I ever had.

Pause.

Should've seen it comin'.

Miles   'Ey.

Errol   My whole life. I'm just a joke, aren't I?

Miles   Not to me yer not. Don't say that, Errol.

Errol   Must be cursed.

Miles   Don't take it out on yerself, don't cry.

Pause.

Don't cry, Errol, she's not worth it, mate. Honest. Honest t'God, yer better off without 'er, yer'll . . .

Errol, *sobbing, embraces* **Miles**.

Miles   Yeah.

He clumsily embraces **Errol**.

Miles   Yeah, that's it, just . . .

Errol   Yer'll stick around won't yer? Tonight?

Miles   'Course.

Errol   Don't know if I can 'andle bein' on me own.

Miles   No. I mean, yeah . . .

Errol   Yer will though won't yer?

Miles   Oh come on, Errol. We're mates, aren't we?

Scene Fourteen

The Peak District. Plateau on the top of a hillside trail. Very high up. Dawn.

Pete *is sitting on a pile of stones (rambler's trail stones).*

Carol *is sleeping on the grass, by the stones. Both their coats are draped over her.*

Long pause.

Pete   Elaine.

He kicks **Carol** *in the arse.*

Elaine.

He kicks **Carol** *in the arse.*

Pete   Wake up.

Carol *wakes.*

Carol   Mmph – wha . . . ?

Pete   Told yer it were beautiful dint I?

Carol *looks around, disorientated.*

Long pause.

Carol   What time is it?

Pete   Fuckin' beautiful.

Carol *lies back down, pulling the coats over her head.*

Pete *kicks her in the arse.*

Carol   Oi!

Pete *whips the coats off her.*

Carol   Pete!

Pete   Yer wanted a surprise dint yer?

Carol *gets up, tries to pull back the coats.* **Pete** *grabs her arm.*

Pete   Wake up.

Carol   But I'm . . .

Pete *slaps her.*

They struggle for a moment, then **Pete** *lets go of* **Carol**.

Carol *stands, stunned, rubbing her face.*

Long pause.

Pete   See this trail? Runs right up through t'downs over
there. Yer see? All through 'ills, alongside Rother forra few
miles, then straight up there through woods. Come out other
side and yer only half hour from Bakewell. Not many people
do this route no more. Too simple. Everyone wants peaks.
Sheer vertical drops up valleys. Nothin' to do with the trail no
more. All about reachin' the top.

Pause.

Used to come 'ere every summer. Ever since I can remember.
Me n'Dad. Like a ritual. 'Get yer boots on, Pete.' There were
times when I dint wanna go. Rather be off smokin' draw
wi'me mates or tekkin' some bird to pictures. I'd mek up any

excuse. Broke me ankle playin' footy, Dad. Can't come,
stitchin's come out kagoul.

Pause.

Always went though dint I? Always dragged me out. 'Rain or
no rain, yer comin'. Get yer boots on.' I remember Miles
n'Gary came with us one time. Draggin' their feet through
the mud n'cursin'. Guess they were too old for all o'that.
Lives to lead, jobs to do. We knew better though, dint we
Dad? Trudgin' through fields like a pair o'soldiers 'eadin'
back to camp. That's what I imagined. You were the captain
and I were private, marchin' through enemy lines. The rocks
were landmines and the sheep were Nazis. And when we got
back home, Mum were gonna give us both medals with us
tea.

Pause.

Not like we ever said owt anyway. Dint need to. Us feet did
all the talkin'.

Pause.

Pete *picks up one of the stones.*

Used to stop off 'ere to eat lunch dint we? Each find a stone
and put it on pile.

He feels the stone in his hands.

Long pause.

Carol *picks up her coat and puts it on.*

Carol   I wanna go 'ome.

Pause.

I wanna go 'ome, Pete.

Pause.

Pete, please . . .

Pete *smacks the stone against his chest.*

Carol   F'fucksake!

Pete *smacks the stone against his chest.*

Carol   Pete!

Pete *smacks the stone against his chest a dozen times.*

Carol *grabs him.*

Carol   Stop it!

Pete *kicks her away, she topples, screams. He repeatedly beats his chest with the stone, drawing blood.*

Carol   Jesus Christ . . .

Pete *continues beating his chest, until both his hand and the stone are covered in blood.*

Carol   Pete, no . . .

She gets up, grabs **Pete***; the stone falls from his hand.*

Carol   Stop it, please, stop . . .

Pete *grabs* **Carol** *by the throat. They struggle for a moment.*

Carol *breaks free.*

Carol   Stupid bloody . . .

She pushes **Pete** *into the stones.*

Look at you!

Scene Fifteen

Kitchen. Morning.

Gary *and* **Elaine** *are sitting at the table, drinking coffee from a coffeepot.*

Elaine *in her dressing gown, holding a bag of frozen peas to her head.*

Gary   'Ow's yer 'angover?

Elaine Oof. Don't ask.

Gary Who were yer out with last night?

Elaine Yer know who I was out with, I told yer. Horse.

Gary Horse?

Elaine Yes, Horse. Don't look at me like that, Gary, I don't need it. Not the way I'm feelin'. 'Ere, give us one o'yer fags and stop bein' so 'orrible.

Gary You don't smoke.

Elaine Look, if it'll take me mind off this headache, I'll smoke 'alf of bloody India if I 'ave to.

Gary Has 'e started all this?

Elaine All this what? Oh, f'Godsake will you stop? It's nine o'clock in the mornin'.

Gary Mum, I near enough 'ad to carry yer home last night! There's puke all over the carpet, on me jeans . . .

Elaine And I suppose that's never happened to you before has it?

Gary I thought yer'd been attacked f'fucksake!

Pause.

Sorry.

Elaine Don't you ever . . .

Gary I said I'm sorry.

Elaine . . . speak to me like that again.

Gary I was worried, that's all.

Elaine You were bein' downright stupid.

Gary Who is this Horse anyway?

Elaine Oh, Jesus Christ . . .

Gary What? I've got a right to know, Mum.

Elaine   Yer worse than Miles with all this racism crap.

Gary   I never said that.

Elaine   He's a mate, Gary. He happens to be Jamaican. He makes me feel good.

Gary   Yeah, right.

Elaine   He makes me feel like a human being, which is a lot more than any of you . . . bloody cretins ever do.

Gary   Bit of a funny name though init? Horse.

Elaine   It's a nickname.

Gary   Bit of a stallion is 'e? Bit of a rogue?

Elaine   Maybe. Maybe 'e's got a great fat twenny-six incher strapped round 'is ankle, I wouldn't know. He's just a friend f'Chrissake. 'E plays dominoes down the East House, 'e's got a guitar, I like 'im. Jesus, anyone'd think yer were me father.

Gary   I just . . .

Pause.

Don't want to see yer make a fool of yerself.

Elaine   What?

Gary   I care about yer.

Elaine   Oh, fuck off!

Gary   Mum!

Elaine   Patronise me. I'm a grown woman.

Gary   I wasn't!

Elaine   Yes you were, you always bloody do! I've seen the looks behind my back. You and yer brother.

Gary   What looks?

Elaine   Like I'm a bloody invalid! Tired worn-out piece of crap, that's me!

Elaine *throws the bag of peas on to the floor. The bag bursts.*

Useless!

Gary   Don't be stupid.

Elaine   Feel like yer'd rather I locked meself away in this stinkin' rat-'ole seven days a week. Keep me out o' harm's way. Better still, send me to the bloody nursin' 'ome, 'ave done with it.

Long pause.

Elaine (*of the peas*)   Oh Christ.

Gary   I don't think like that, Mum. You know I don't. We love you. The three of us. It's just . . . I don't wanna watch yer get hurt.

Elaine   Oh God. Don't you ever listen? I'm fine, Gary. Look at me. Well, not now, but . . . I'm happy. It's good for me all this.

Gary   All this what?

Elaine   Can't you see, I'm tired of this place. I'm tired, Gary. It's good f'me to get out. Even if it's just once of a Thursday, it's right, it's . . .

Long pause.

Look, I can see yer've not been well.

Gary   Eh?

Elaine   It's written all over yer face. Ever since yer split up with Sophie. Before that even, when yer dad died, God rest his soul.

Gary   I don't see 'ow . . .

Elaine   Sometimes yer just need to make the change, son. Put the past to rest, start again. Yer gonna be down London in a couple o'months. It's gonna get better, I promise.

Gary   Yeah . . .

Elaine   I promise yer, Gary, yer'll see.

Long pause.

Bloody peas.

Long pause.

Gary   Mum . . .

Elaine   'Ere, let's just forget about it, eh? I'm sorry I snapped, it's not . . .

Gary   I'm not goin'. To London. I'm not goin'. I rang up the college before yer got up. Cancelled my place. Said they could give it to somebody else. It's not like they're short of applicants anyway.

Pause.

Elaine   Are you . . .

Gary   I cunt do it, Mum. Kept thinkin' about you n'Miles n'Pete. I'm needed 'ere. I can't just walk away. Don't even know why I did it in first place.

Elaine   Oh, Gary.

Gary   Thought I'd better tell yer anyway.

Elaine   You idiot.

Gary   Just wcrcn't for me, Mum.

Elaine   And what is right for you?

Gary   This place o'course. You n'Miles n' . . .

Elaine   You're thirty years old, son.

Gary   I know. I know that.

Elaine   Yer can't stay here for ever.

Gary   I just dint . . .

Elaine   I don't believe this.

Gary   All right . . .

Elaine   I don't believe you, Gary. A chance like that and yer just throw it away like a piece of old rubbish? What's wrong with you? Yer lettin' life pass yer by, son, f'Godssake.

Gary   I need to be here don't I? For you n' . . .

Elaine   Stop sayin' that. Need to be here? Jesus Christ, look at yer. Sat there like an old man already. Can't even remember the last time yer laughed, or cracked a joke, or . . . Hidin' away like a shadow day in, day out, it breaks my heart. What's happened?

Pause.

What's happened, Gary, eh?

Long pause.

That bitch.

Gary   What?

Elaine   It's her fault, all this. Sophie bleedin' whats-er-name.

Gary   Don't you call 'er that.

Elaine   I'll call her what I like, I don't owe 'er no apology. If it wasn't for 'er, you wouldn't even be 'ere.

Gary   She is not a bitch.

Elaine   Knew it from the moment I clapped eyes on 'er. Schemin' little toad. Couldn't wait to flee the nest once she'd bled yer dry.

Gary   It wasn't like that. You didn't even know 'er, Mum.

Elaine   Then why'd she run off like that?

Gary   'Cause. It just wasn't 'appenin', you weren't there.

Elaine   Another bloody five years flushed down the toilet.

Gary   Jesus Christ, . . .

Elaine   While she flaunts herself all over the country . . .

Gary   It's got nothin' to do with it, Mum! If anythin' it was my fault.

Elaine   She didn't care about you.

Gary   Mum!

Elaine   She didn't care about anyone! Couldn't even manage to drag 'erself to the funeral, when you needed 'er. Where was she then, eh? . . . Well?

Gary   She 'ad an audition.

Elaine   Audition.

Gary   She did.

Elaine   Waste o'bloody space. I'm not 'avin' it, 'ear?

Gary   Well it's nice to know I've got yer support, Mum, thanks.

Elaine   You just don't get it do yer?

Gary   All I'm doin' is thinkin' of the family.

Elaine   The family?

Gary   Well someone's got to! You don't, that's for sure.

Elaine   Yes I do, I . . .

Gary   Oh come on.

Elaine   You're the only thing I've got f'Chrissake!

Gary   Oh yeah? When was the last time you went to see Pete, eh? Yer think I'm fucked up, yer should see 'im! 'E won't even talk to me no more! 'Im and Miles had a fight the other week! Dint know that did yer? 'E needs us, Mum, they both do! Miles lost 'is job down the buildin' site; I thought 'e were gonna flip! Now what's gonna happen if I go down London? Who's 'e gonna turn to then? Dad?

Elaine   Yer dad's dead, Gary.

Gary   Oh, that's funny, I thought it'd slipped yer mind.

Elaine   How dare you . . .

Gary   Wunt surprise me. Sat in the pub like a cheap dirty slag drinkin' fuckin' tequilas all . . .

Elaine   Get out!

Gary (*stands*)   Yeah . . .

Elaine   Go on! Fuck off!

Gary   Truth hurts dunt it?

Elaine   Out my 'ouse, now!

Gary *exits.*

Elaine   Bastard! Fuckin' . . .

Pause.

Stupid fuckin' bastard.

Scene Sixteen

Hillside trail. Morning.

Carol *and* **Pete** *are walking down a craggy slope, on the trail.*

Carol *holds tightly onto* **Pete**, *whose chest and hand are stained with blood.*

Carol   Are you all right? D'yer want to stop forra bit?

Pete *shakes his head.*

They keep walking.

Pause.

Carol   I'm gonna call an ambulance when we get back to car.

They keep walking.

Pause.

I'm gonna . . .

Pete *stops, grabs his chest.*

Pete   Aah.

Carol   You all right?

Pete   Yeah. Yeah, I'm . . . fine.

He starts walking again, **Carol** *holding him.*

Pause.

Carol   Frightened the life outta me.

They keep walking.

Pause.

Yer don't mind d'yer?

Pete   What?

Carol   If I go back 'ome forra bit.

Pause.

Just forra bit. Me mum'll be worried sick. Probably got the cops out n'everythin'. Search parties. (*Laughs.*) Can you imagine?

Pete *stops for a moment, rubbing his chest.*

Pause.

Carol   I mean. That's all right init, Pete?

Pete   Weren't s'pposed to 'appen like this.

Carol   Just say I'd been at Becky's or somert.

Pete   Should've ended it.

Carol   I don't think they've got 'er number.

Pete   Me n'you, on top. I saw it. Lyin' on top o'the pile, in me 'ead. Then later. Under the tree. Side be side. Just like 'im.

Carol Silly sod. What we gonna do with you, eh? Should know better than that. There's people out there can 'elp yer, yer know?

Pause.

Pete . . .

Pete Yeah, I know.

Carol Yer not even listenin'. Yer never listen to me.

Pete No. I could listen to you for hours.

Carol Some bloody surprise.

Carol *escorts* **Pete** *along the trail.*

Pause.

Probably think I 'ad it planned all along. Cunt understand why I dint wanna go. Put it down to hormones or somert. Too old for all that aren't I? Got me own life t'lead 'ant I, Pete? Both of us.

They walk.

Pause.

Who is Donald anyway?

Pete What?

Carol Yer know. Donald Duck.

Scene Seventeen

Pub. Day. Music.

Miles *and* **Errol** *are playing pool.*

Miles Yer know, I was wrong about you, Ezzer. Used to think, well . . . Used to think you were just like all the others. Not like I've ever really known any blacks or owt before. Not to chat to anyway. Not like this. Just normal n'that. Where yer from again? Originally like?

Errol   Sheffield. I were born in Sheffield.

Miles   No, originally originally.

Errol   Northern General Hospital.

Miles   No, I mean . . .

Errol   Where me parents from?

Miles   Yeah, if yer like.

Errol   Well me dad's from Somalia, n'me mum's from Doncaster.

Miles   Doncaster?

Errol   Yeah.

Miles   England Doncaster?

Errol   Yeah.

Miles   What? Moved over did she?

Errol   Eh?

Miles   From Sumatra n'that.

Errol   No, she's British int she. I'm mixed race. Can't yer tell?

Miles   She's white?

Errol   I thought yer knew. It's obvious int it?

Miles   Oh.

Errol *takes a shot, pots.*

Pause.

Errol   Good game this. Pool. What with all the different colours n'that.

Miles (*laughs*)   What is this, fuckin' 'playschool'?

Pause.

Oh, right. See what yer mean. Like us n'that.

Pause.

Errol 'Ey, listen. Thanks for last night. Thanks for 'elpin' me through all . . .

Miles Oh! Don't worry about it.

Errol No, but really, I don't know what I'd done without . . .

Miles Ezzer, please. It were nothin'.

Errol Best forty quid I've ever spent.

Miles Plenty more where that came from n'all. Fuckin' ace idea, mate. Can see it now. Painted across van. Miles & Errol, hire us at your peril.

Errol Yer definitely up for it then?

Miles Oh yeah, think it's a crackin' idea. We'll make a packet, what wi' your contacts, my contacts. Just need the tools really. Bit o' nifty advertisin' in *Star*, and bingo. It'll be us two jet-settin' round Spain next year. Hire as many babysitters as yer like then – I mean, just think about it. Already got most the capital anyway, what with the money from me dad. I mean, I've gotta use it for somert though 'ant I?

Errol What about the council tax?

Miles Ach. Ways n'means, Ezzer, ways n'means.

Errol Yer sure yer don't mind?

Miles Yeah, well a bit o'give n'take won't go amiss. But, fuck it, five–ten years down the line, could be makin' fuckin' thousands. It'll all be worth it in end. Swear to God, give it a month, yer'll have forgotten all about that slut. Wunt be surprised if she comes crawlin' back anyway, yer know what they're like. Seriously. Yer should be like me. Free n'single with the pick of the litter. If I dint 'ave me 'ead screwed on, I could o'had thirty sprogs be now. Dunt bother me, women. 'Appy as I am.

Errol Glad to 'ear it.

Miles Not that I'm a puff or owt.

Errol Just take yer shot will yer?

Miles *stands, staring at* **Errol**, *smiling.*

Pause.

Errol What?

Miles Dunno. Just . . . Feel different, yer know? Like . . . Nowt matters no more. None of it. Everythin' I've been through the last God knows how long, it . . . It's like it weren't even real.

Errol Well that's all right then init?

Miles Yeah it is. Thanks to you.

Errol Yer gonna take us out clubbin' then?

Scene Eighteen

Graveyard. The father's headstone. Day.

Elaine *is standing by the headstone, holding a bunch of flowers.*

Long pause.

Elaine Donald? Donald, it's me. Elaine.

Pause.

Bloody 'ell. It's been a while 'asn't it? Never one for flowers were yer? I 'ope yer don't mind.

She lays the flowers before the headstone.

Bring a cactus next time, eh?

Long pause.

Well. What is there to tell?

Pause.

TV's still up the spout. Keep gettin' Five instead o'Four. Was gonna get it fixed, but, yer know?

Pause.

I 'ad this girl come round the other day from On digital, tryin' to sell me some bloody rubbish. Apparently we've all gotta start usin' the Internet now. Way of the future, she said, yer'll be lost without it. Thought to myself, 'What do you know about lost?'. Sweet little thing looked at me like I was mad. Oh yeah, yer probably wonderin' about my hair aren't yer? Very Diana Dors, eh?

Long pause.

That cat still comes round from next door. Cinnamon. Leavin' 'is little gifts for me to clean up. What else?

Pause.

Oh yeah, Gary fixed that bike of yours. The old racer. He's been with us – with me, I should say, the last year or so. Had a bit of a bust-up with Sophie. You remember 'er, don't yer? The actress.

Pause.

Bit too common for the likes of 'er weren't we? But . . . You know Gary. Heart like a flannel. Still loves 'er to bits, even after everythin'.

Pause.

Miles is just the same. Floatin'.

Pause.

And Pete? Well, I guess yer've already spoke to 'im by now.

Long pause.

They seem to think I've forgotten you. God knows I've tried.

Long pause.

Funny how all you remember is the good stuff. It's like the rest never existed. The arguments, the depression, the drink, . . . I haven't told them, if that's what you're thinkin'. All those weekends away. Your so-called conferences, trainin' days, Jesus Christ, I'd almost forgot myself. Dirty bastard. Dirty filthy rotten . . .

Pause.

Well. What's done is done.

Pause.

At least it wasn't painful, eh? In the end.

Long pause.

They've done this research? Somewhere in America, I saw it on the news the other day. Breakthrough research in genetics. DNA whatsit strands, it's all nonsense to me. Well, anyway, it seems they might have found a cure. Or rather, they're trying to find a cure. Something about replacement cells or some such. Anyway I was watching this programme, and I thought of you and I . . .

Pause.

If you were still here and they did . . . manage to find a cure. I mean . . . Regardless of everything. Everything we went through together. In the hospital week after week, the pain you went – we all went through.

Pause.

Like it was destiny or something. Like it was God reachin' down and . . . touching us somehow.

Pause.

I don't know.

Long pause.

I need yer to let me go, Donald. I'm drownin'.

Scene Nineteen

Pete's *bedroom. The following day.*

Pete *is sitting on the edge of the bed, his chest bandaged. He shuffles a deck of cards in his hand.*

Knock on the door.

Gary (*off*)   Pete? Can I come in?

Gary *enters.*

I'm goin' down the shops. D'yer want anythin'?

Pause.

I'll take that as a no then, yeah?

Pete   Wunt mind some fruit.

Gary   Fruit.

Pete   Yeah. Mango. Couple o'mangos.

Gary   I don't think they're that exotic down Mr King's. Might get a tin o'manky peaches or somert.

Pause.

'Ere, bit dark in 'ere int it? Ever thought about openin' the curtains?

Pause.

'Ere.

Gary *moves across the room, opens the curtains, light shines in.*

That's more like it. Anyone'd think we were in Transylvania.

Pause.

Dracula like.

Pete   Yeah?

Gary   Yeah, I mean . . .

Pause.

I'll tidy up a bit if yer like. While I'm 'ere. Bring the hoover from Mum's. Suck up all the ants. Clean the piss off the toilet.

Pause.

Wi'me pinny on n'that.

Pause.

'Ere, I'll even bring video over if yer want. Make a night of it. Few films like.

Pete   Yeah?

Gary   Bloody 'ell, Pete, so you 'ave got some life in yer after all.

Pete   What films?

Gary   Owt yer like. Got tons o'films me 'ant I?

Pete   Yer got *Godfather*?

Gary   'Ave I got *The Godfather*. I've got the fuckin' box set, mate. Best American films ever made. Them n'*Taxi Driver*. Do a session if yer like. Scorsese n'Coppola, from *Boxcar Bertha* to *Ragin' Bull*. Tell yer what, I'll even throw in a bit o'Kurosawa.

Pete   Who?

Gary   Kurosawa. 'E's Japanese. Akira Kurosawa.

Pete   What, like manga?

Gary   Fuck manga, this is real cinema, mate. *Throne of Blood*, *Seven Samurai*, *Ran*. Honest t'God, Pete, it's like Shakespeare. And the cinematography, Jesus Christ. I mean, there's shots in *Throne o'Blood*, right? Like, nothin' shots. Bit o'tree wi'the clouds passin' by. Mist creepin' over the hills, yer know? Like

in the 'ands of anyone else they'd be just nothin', right? Yer
wunt even register them. But Kurosawa, mate. It's like fuckin'
poetry. Like magic. Like . . . It's not just mist, yer know? It's .
. . it's . . . It's *mist*. It's frightenin'. It's the witches comin' out
the forest and mergin' with the elements and . . . What?
Don't look at me like that.

Pete   Weirdo.

Gary   Weirdo? It's a cinematic masterpiece, Pete.

Pete   Oh. Wunt know.

Long pause.

Gary   What's them yer got there? Cards?

Pete   Did yer want a game?

Gary   What, now?

Pete   You brought it up.

Gary   'Ant played cards in ages.

Pete   Play yerra game o' shit'ead if yer want. Loser makes
brews.

Gary   I were just about to get dinner in.

Pete   Pussy.

Gary   What?

Pete   What I said. Pussy.

Gary   Fuckin' gimme them!

Gary *grabs the cards, sits down on the bed.*

Put pillow down then. Need a deck init? Can't play shit'ead
wi'out a decent deck.

Pete *puts a pillow between him and* **Gary**.

Gary *shuffles the cards.*

Gary I'll show you pussy, fuckin' . . . Jesus Christ, I will n'all!

Gary *scans through the cards.*

Pete What?

Gary You dirty bastard, Peter. Kept these a bit quiet dint yer? Jesus (*Laughs.*) . . . Look at that! (*Laughs.*) They can't be real.

Gary *scans through the cards, laughing.*

No! No way!

Pete *starts to laugh at* **Gary**.

Gary D'yer think they're all the same family or somert? . . . Jesus Christ, that's not possible is it? . . . Fucks up theory o' gravity that one, look . . . 'Ere, look!

Gary *bursts out laughing.*

Look, no!

Pete (*laughing*) What?

Gary No, it can't be, it . . .

Pete What? Give it us will yer?

Gary (*shows him the card*) Fuckin' Miles, look!

Pete Let's see, come on!

Pete *grabs the card, laughs.*

Gary It's 'im int it? Miles! It's Miles, look! But wi' big bloody bazookers!

Gary *and* **Pete** *laugh.*

Init though? Init 'im?

Scene Twenty

Kitchen. The following week. Early evening.

Elaine *is ironing.*

Miles *is sitting at the kitchen table, very despondent.*

The table is laid with four plates and cutlery. On the table is **Errol**'*s wooden African head, still broken in two pieces.* **Miles** *trying to balance the two pieces together. It falls apart.*

Miles   Fuck it.

Elaine   Look, are you gonna be like this all day?

Miles *tries fixing the two pieces together again. It falls apart.*

Elaine   Miles!

Miles   What?

Elaine   I've already told yer, leave it alone. I know yer upset, just . . .

Miles   Upset's not the word, Mum. I'm fuckin', I'm fuckin' . . .

Elaine   Upset.

Miles   Can't believe it.

Elaine   Well, yer've only got yerself to blame.

Miles   But . . .

Elaine   Throwin' away yer savin's like that. How could yer be so stupid?

Miles   I know.

Elaine   Yer must've suspected somethin'.

Miles   Does it look like it? We grew up together f'fucksake! Well, sort of. Used to play bulldog in the park. My mates n'is mates.

Elaine   Oh, Miles. Yer never change do yer?

Miles   I trusted 'im, Mum. Little bastard poured his heart out to me.

Elaine   Well there's nothin' hard about that.

Miles   All that time, the prick. 'E must've planned it all along. Fuckin' Spaniards and business enterprises and two-timin' bloody wives. That's blackmail that. Emotional blackmail.

Elaine   Does nobody know where he is?

Miles   Oh yeah, I know where he is, all right? Livin' it up in Grand fuckin' Canaria. Him and his wife and their shitty-arsed little baby. Five thousand quid, gone. Like it never even happened. Went down the site to see if anybody knew anythin'. D'yer know what I found?

Miles *pulls out one of* **Errol***'s polaroids from his jeans. He shows it to* **Elaine***.*

Miles   Happy bleedin' families, right?

Elaine   Is that them?

Miles   Yeah. Notice anythin' peculiar?

Elaine   No, not . . .

Pause.

Unless. Is that – through the window there? – Is that the sea?

Miles   It's Spain, Mum. Look at it. The three of them in Spain. The writin' on the cereal box, look. Spanish. His wife even, look.

Elaine   Got a lovely tan 'ant she?

Miles   Tan? The woman's Spanish, Mum! Look at 'er! That's yer classic Spanish bint! I asked the foreman if he knew anythin' about 'im. At the site? Seems 'e's been livin' there for the past six years, but is work permit fell through. 'Ad to come back 'ere, sort 'imself out, raise a bit o'money. Why d'yer think 'e never got the sack when I did? Bastards took pity on 'im. No wonder I was so surprised when 'e just turned up out the blue. Prick 'ant been in the country for years.

Long pause.

Was gonna be great n'all. Our little business. I 'ad it all planned out. Could o'bloody worked too. Cunt believe it when I went round. We were s'pposed to be goin' over the publicity campaign. But who answers the door? His bloody sister in 'er dressing gown. Wasn't even 'is yard. Sly sod'd been kippin' on the floor for three months while he planned it all out. 'He's gone back to Spain,' she says. 'He left this mornin', dint 'e say?' I'm like, 'no'. 'Oh yeah, he come into some money apparently. Caught the train to Manchester this mornin'. Booked himself a plane ticket.' Swear to God, Mum, I thought I were gonna faint. She must've thought I were a right dippy twat. Stood on the doorstep like a stray dog lookin' for bones.

Pause.

Dint even leave us a note.

Long pause.

Five thousand quid.

Elaine   Well let's face it, Miles. Yer probably would've just wasted it on beer anyway.

Miles   Yeah, well, it's the principle init?

Long pause.

Still gonna do it though. Once I get me council tax sorted.

Elaine   What's that, love?

Miles   Dunt that Horse 'ave a van?

Elaine   My Horse?

Miles   'E's drivin' you all to Skeggy next week int 'e?

Elaine   Well, yes, but . . .

Miles   In 'is van.

Elaine   Look, Miles love . . .

Miles   D'yer think 'e'd fancy bein' a partner? Nothin' major like. I mean, I'll get all the tools.

Elaine   One thing at a time.

Miles   Oh, come on, Mum, it'd be great. I'll ask 'im meself if yer'd rather.

There is a knock at the door, offstage.

Elaine   Oh. That'll be yer brothers.

Elaine *exits.*

Pause.

Miles *tries for the very last time to stick the statue together. It holds.* **Miles** *smiles at his handiwork.*

Enter **Elaine**, *followed by* **Pete** *and* **Gary**. **Pete** *carries a bag of laundry in a bin liner.*

Elaine (*as they enter*)   . . . just finished the bloody ironin'. 'Ere, sit down, sit down.

Pete *and* **Gary** *sit at the table.*

Over the following, **Elaine** *takes* **Pete**'s *bag of laundry and puts it away with the ironing board. She then opens the oven door, and using a couple of tea-towels, removes a steaming dish of lasagne.*

Pete (*as they sit*)   You all right?

Miles (*indicates statue*)   Good init?

Gary   What?

Miles   This.

Pete   Blimey, Miles, yer did that all by yerself? I never 'ad you as a sculptor.

Miles   I'm not on about the bloody . . .

Gary   Leonardo daVinci 'ere.

Miles   Yeah, all right, yer can laugh all yer want . . .

The statue falls apart.

Pete *and* **Gary** *laugh.*

Miles   You n'yer big bloody mouth!

Pete *and* **Gary** *laugh.*

Miles (*laughs*)   Gi'over will yer?

Elaine   Now, I hope yer all hungry.

Gary   Arrrr, Mum.

Elaine *moves to the table with the dish of lasagne. Appetising groans from the boys.*

Elaine   Clear a space will yer, Pete, there's a good boy.

Pete   That smells great, Mum.

Elaine   Miles, keep yer 'ands out.

Miles   I'm not!

Elaine (*placing the dish on the table*)   There we go now.

Elaine *sits at the table. The meal begins.*

Long pause.

Elaine   Well. This is nice.

Redundant

Redundant was first performed at the Royal Court Theatre
Downstairs, on 6 September 2001. The cast was as follows:

Lucy	Lyndsey Marshal
Darren	Simon Trinder
Dave	Wil Johnson
Gonzo	Craig Heaney
Nikki	Rachel Brogan
Jo	Eileen O'Brien

Directed by Dominic Cooke
Designed by Robert Innes Hopkins
Lighting by Peter Mumford
Sound by Gareth Fry

Characters

Lucy, *seventeen years old, white*
Darren, *seventeen years old, black*
Nikki, *sixteen years old, Lucy's sister, mixed race*
Dave, *thirty-two years old, black*
Gonzo, *twenty-three years old, white*
Jo, *sixty years old, Lucy's gran, white*

Setting:

Sheffield. Between December 1999 and December 2000.

Lucy's council flat, third/top floor. Lounge/bedroom.
Front door, leading to stairway. Alcove leading to bathroom
and a kitchen. One window with curtains. Grotty double bed,
near the window. Small old portable television. Small
tapedeck. Box of tapes. No telephone. No carpet. Floor is
covered with lino. Old chest of drawers, stuffed with clothes.
On top of the chest are cosmetics and cheap jewellery, a
small mirror and a small framed photo of a small baby.
Damp yellow walls. Poster of Bob Marley. Old electric heater
fitted into the wall. Some kind of seating: cushions, beanbags,
the odd crappy chair perhaps. The flat should be cluttered
with clothes and various junk.

Scene One

Night. December.
The heater is off.
Lucy *stands by the window, looking out.*
Darren *sits on the sofa, eating chips and battered sausage with his hands.*

Lucy   Reckon it'll snow this year?

Pause.

Can't 'member last time it snowed.

Darren   Too wet f'snow. Evaporates on its way down like.

Lucy   All smog n'that?

Darren   Yeah.

Lucy   I know. Not like when we wa' kids. Did yer ever go sledgin' or owt?

Darren   Oh aye, all time. Just over down whatsit, Ecclesall Park n'that. Loads en'us on plastic bags bombin' it down 'ill. Used t'love it. Snow fights, sledgin'.

Lucy   Ever build a snowman?

Darren   Oh aye.

Lucy   No yer never. Only girls build snowmen.

Darren   Eh?

Lucy   Only girls build snowmen.

Darren   Naow.

Lucy   Must be a puff. Uuuuuur.

Darren   Naow, only when I were little. Wi'me sisters n'that.

Lucy   I jus' like watchin' it me. Like the way it covers everythin' up, so yer can't tell what's what.

Pause. She shuts the curtains.

You alright?

Darren   Yeah. Nice place.

Lucy   Liar.

Darren   No I'm not. Cosy int it?

Lucy   Could do with a clean. Messy cow me.

Darren   Me too.

Lucy   Messy bastard yer mean.

Darren   Yeah.

Lucy   Need a butler. Bloody Jeeves or somert. Wash me pots.

Darren   Should see me bedroom back 'ome.

Lucy   Dint think yer'd come.

Darren   'Course. Somert t'do, int it?

Lucy   Bit borin' like. Should o'brought some cards really. I'd o'got a couple o'board games if I'd known. Gran's got 'ole box o'games back 'ome. Guess 'oo. Buckaroo. Operation. Monopoly.

Darren   I like Cluedo me. Colonel Mustard.

Lucy   Colonel Custard.

Darren   All of 'em. Miss Scarlet.

Lucy   In the conservatory.

Darren   Wi'lead pipin' like, bosh.

Lucy   Do that again.

Darren   Eh?

Lucy   What yer did just then. Lead pipin'.

Darren   Oh. Bosh.

Lucy   You're funny you.

Pause.

Not too bored are yer?

Darren   I'm not bored.

Lucy   No, but once yer've lived 'ere a bit. Starin' at box all day.

She sits next to **Darren**.

Lucy   I like yer trainers. They new?

Darren   Yeah.

Lucy   Where d'yer get 'em?

Darren   Town.

Lucy   I like 'em. Adidas. I like the colour n'that.

Darren   D'yer?

Lucy   Yeah. They suit yer.

Darren   Love me trainers me.

Lucy   What size o'they?

Darren   Eh?

Lucy   Can I try 'em on?

Darren   What fu'?

Lucy   Somert t'do init. What size o'they?

Darren   Eight.

Lucy   Gi'em us.

Darren   Too big f'you.

Lucy   No they're not, go on. Jus' forra sec like.

Darren *hesitates, then takes off his trainers.*

Lucy *takes them.*

Lucy   Must o'cost a bit.

Darren   Thirty quid. Knocked down from forty.

Lucy   Smart.

She puts on the trainers.

'Ey, they're alright these, aren't they?

She stands with the trainers.

Bouncy.

Lucy *walks round the flat, testing the trainers. Starts bouncing up and down on the spot.*

Darren   Gi'oer Lucy, yer'll wreck the soles.

Lucy   What Tiggers do best though int it? Can I keep 'em?

Darren   Eh? Yer jokin', aren't yer? I only bought 'em other day.

Lucy   Yeah, but they look better on me than they do you.

Darren   N'what am I gonna wear?

Lucy   Be an early Christmas present like.

Darren   No chance.

Lucy *sits next to* **Darren**.

Lucy   Suit me though, don't they? Don't they?

Pause.

Darren   Bit cold in 'ere int it?

Lucy   No one's forcin' yer to stay.

She moves to the heater and turns it on.

Said they were gonna fix us radiators. Bloody council. S'pposed to be doin' whole block like. Lazy bastards. You got radiators at your place?

Darren   Couple.

Lucy   I'm on a gas card me. Got a lekky key n'all.
Nightmare at Christmas.

Darren   Want some chips? Loaded wi'vinegar mind. Love
me vinegar me. Vinegar crackers.

Lucy   You eat funny don't yer?

Darren   Eh? No I don't.

Lucy   Funny like a camel. 'Ere, yer dint buy 'em from
Chinky did yer?

Darren   Down parade there?

Lucy   Yer did dint yer? Oh naow.

Darren   What?

Lucy   Shunt go there yer know?

Darren   Why not?

Lucy   'E wanks in batter.

Darren   'Oo?

Lucy   That Mr Fu. 'E wanks in batter.

Darren   No 'e dunt.

Lucy   Does.

Darren   No 'e dunt. Really?

Lucy   Yeah. Common knowledge that.

Darren   Since when?

Lucy   Since 'is car got robbed.

Darren   Eh?

Lucy   Dave told us. There were pubes in 'is fish cake.

Darren   Naow.

Lucy   That's 'ow they know, like. 'Ow else do they get there? 'E's a racist bastard that Mr Fu. Dunt like yer 'less yer fuckin' Chinky. Thinks we're all out t'rob 'im or somert. Bin there yonks n'all. Think 'e'd 'ave more sense.

Darren   Spunk?

Lucy   Yeah.

Darren   'E spunks up? Fuck that.

He wraps his chips up in the paper.

Fuck that. Uuurgh.

Lucy   I go by Blockbusters now.

Darren   Should get me stomach pumped.

Lucy   Burger King. Double whopper wi'cheese. Onion rings on giro day.

Darren   Could o'told me before.

Lucy   Thought yer knew.

Darren   Oh man!

He stands.

Quick, where's yer bog?

Lucy   Not gonna be sick, are yer?

Darren   No, jus' . . .

Darren *moves through the alcove, exits into the toilet.*

Lucy *spots a toothbrush poking out of* **Darren***'s jacket pocket. She takes it out, stands, moves to the alcove.*

Darren *re-enters.*

Lucy   Lookin' for this?

Darren   Yeah. Cheers.

Darren *exits into the bathroom.*

Lucy *moves over to the cassette player, presses play. Music comes on, Bob Marley.* **Lucy** *exits into the kitchen.*

Darren *re-enters, holding the toothbrush. He sits and puts the toothbrush back in the jacket.*

Lucy *re-enters with two cans of lager.*

Lucy   You plannin' on stayin' the night?

Darren   Oh no, I . . .

Lucy *throws a can to* **Darren**, *who catches it.*

Darren   Tek it to work with us like.

Lucy   Yer can if yer like.

Pause.

Lucy *straightens her bed.* **Darren** *drinks from the can.*

Lucy   Sleep on floor n'that.

Pause.

Darren   You, er . . . Yer seein' anyone or anyone?

Lucy   What?

Darren   I 'eard about you n'Mr Lewis. Got sack in end dint 'e?

Lucy   Don't be so nosy. Nosy. Worse than them gets downstairs. Said yer could stop over, that's all.

Darren   Sorry. 'Ant seen yer 'ave I?

Pause.

Lucy   Cheeky chops.

She sits by **Darren**.

Never change do yer? Remember at school yer were always flappin' 'bout somethin' someone told yer. Like Hislop when 'e said 'e 'ad cancer that time. Or when yer thought yer'd seen that ghost.

Darren   Naow.

Lucy   Yes yer did, I remember. In the physics lab.

Darren   Only forra week.

Lucy (*sings*)   Scaredy-cat, scaredy-cat, sittin' on the doormat.

Darren   Naow. It were just a shadow like. Weren't real.

Long pause.

Lucy   D'yer like Bob Marley?

Darren   'E's alright.

Lucy   Can't beat Bob, mate. Proper spiritual, aren't they? The songs. Could listen to 'im for hours. Like 'e's not dead, like 'e's bricked up in walls n'callin' out through plaster. Like Jesus.

Darren   Prefer R'n'B n'that. Destiny's Child. Brandy.

Lucy   I reckon 'e was Jesus. That's why 'e died so young.

Darren   Don't be stupid.

Lucy   Dave can't stand 'im. 'E's got shit taste in music, Dave. (*Pause.*) Me boyfriend like.

Darren   Oh.

Pause.

Lucy   You alright?

Darren   Yeah. Fine.

Lucy   'E's not like you. Dunt work like you.

Darren   Eh?

Lucy   Does me nut in. Treats me like dirt.

Darren   Oh. Should say somert.

Lucy   Yeah. I might n'all. Thanks.

Darren   S'alright.

Lucy   You're nice you.

Pause.

Yer got work tomorrow?

Darren   Yeah. Wi'me uncle n'that.

Lucy   Must be doin' well f'yersen now.

Darren   Bin there ages now. Big job like. Gonna be great
when it opens. Proper recordin' studio. F'the community,
like. Massive n'all. 'Ad to totally rip place apart at first.
Fuckin' rats everywhere.

Lucy   Uuur.

Darren   I know. Big fat things. Come up from chicken
shop like. Tails like that. 'Ad to knock 'em on 'ead with me
'ammer.

Lucy   Good money though. New pair o'trainers every week.

Darren   Seen this? Tommy Hilfiger like.

Lucy   That's good then, int it? Used to be a right scruffy sod
at school.

Darren   I know. Needed shootin'.

Lucy   Yer gonna take the day off tomorrow?

Darren   Jokin', aren't yer?

Lucy   There's a pub round the corner. Don't ask for ID or
owt. Go together cunt we?

Darren   Me dad'd go mad, Luce. Sorry.

Pause.

Lucy   Felt weird, dint it? Other day. Of all the bloody
people.

Darren   I know. Good though.

Lucy   Just weird warnt it? All this time n'suddenly . . . 'Ere we are. Bosh.

Darren   Wi'lead pipin' n'that.

Lucy (*eagerly*)   Yeah. Dint think yer'd come.

Pause.

Could just say yer sick.

Darren   Delivery at ten.

Lucy   Never used t'stop yer before. 'Member they put you on one o'them report cards.

Darren   That were then though warnt it?

Lucy   That were then though warnt it?

Darren   Naow.

Lucy   Dint like school much did yer?

Darren   Were alright.

Lucy   Cunt stand it mesen. Never wagged it though. Not like you. What yer do? Used t'go off on yer own dint yer?

Darren   Not always.

Lucy   Wunt 'ave bottle, me.

Darren   Used to catch bus t'Barnsley like. Go the pictures. There were only ever me in there n'all. Could 'ave a fag n'everythin'.

Lucy   Honest?

Darren   'Member watchin' *Alien Resurrection* 'bout five times. Brilliant it wa'. Getting' into an eighteen n'that. There were this pub I used to go to. In Chapeltown. Sit n'ave a couple o'pints n'listen t'me Walkman.

Lucy   Alky.

Darren   I weren't no alky, that's just what everyone thought. I were only fourteen anyway. (*Pause.*) Don't ever think about it no more.

Lucy   Dint yer get bored?

Darren   Not really. Long as there were somert to watch. Better than school.

Lucy   Bit o'freedom, yeah?

Darren   Yeah.

Lucy   I like that.

Darren   Yeah?

Lucy   Yeah.

Darren   Fuckin' Barnsley though, int it?

Lucy   Yeah.

Pause.

Always thought yer fancied us.

Pause.

Weren't like all the others, were yer?

Pause.

Is it true what they said? When yer were sick that time? Why yer cunt do PE no more?

Pause.

Did it 'urt?

Pause.

Darren   What time's last bus?

Lucy   'Bout five past.

Darren   It's five past now.

Lucy   Best get goin' then, 'ant yer?

Darren   Gi'us me trainers.

Lucy   Can't I keep 'em?

Darren   No.

Pause.

Lucy   'E's not comin' back.

Darren   Eh?

Lucy   Dave. E's in Amsterdam at moment. 'Im n'is mate Gonzo. They saved up these coupons off *Sun*. Fuckin' thinks 'e's Denzel Washington or somert. Big bastard like that. Not like you.

Darren   Oh.

Lucy   Put a few pounds on 'ant yer?

Darren   Naow.

Lucy   Jelly belly.

Darren   Must be me mum's cookin' like.

Lucy   I like it though. Looks cute.

Darren   Karen 'ates it.

Lucy   Karen?

Darren   Yeah. Me girlfriend. Me girlfriend, Karen.

Lucy   Since when?

Darren   Few month back.

Lucy   Liar.

Darren   Lives down our road. Comes from Derby. Loaded she is. Got 'er own car n'that. Volvo.

Lucy   Oh. Nice girl, yeah?

Darren   Yeah. Yeah, she is a bit.

Pause.

Lucy   Funny that. I thought you were a virgin still.

Darren   Eh?

Lucy   Yer look like a virgin.

Darren   Don't be stupid.

Lucy   She good in bed?

Darren   What?

Lucy   Karen. She good in bed?

Darren   Yeah, she's . . . She's fine.

Lucy   That's good then, int it? Remember at school. Fretty. Best mates at one point, weren't yer?

Darren   Not really.

Lucy   Ren n'bloody Stimpy. Actin' up t'tatchers.

Darren   Only in first year.

Lucy   Said 'e taught you 'ow to wank.

Darren   Eh?

Lucy   Said yer used to camp out in 'is backyard and 'e told ycr to imagine someone. Like yer'd never 'ad an 'ard-on before.

Darren   No I dint.

Lucy   'E said you imagined me.

Darren   You?

Lucy   But yer cunt cum or somert. Like it weren't developed enough.

Darren   Yer dint believe 'im, did yer?

Lucy   Yer ever wank over Karen? You 'ant, 'ave yer?

Darren   No.

Lucy   But yer did over me.

Darren   Course not.

Lucy   Yes yer did. I know yer did.

Pause.

Does she even know yer 'ere?

Darren   No, she's . . . She's at church.

Lucy   Never.

Darren   That's where I met 'er like.

Lucy   Oh my God. You never go fuckin' church.

Darren   Yeah. Course. Pentecostal like.

Lucy   All that gospel crap?

Darren   No it's not.

Lucy   Fuckin' crap.

Darren   Same as 'im.

Lucy   'Oo?

Darren   Bob bloody Marley. Same as 'im.

Lucy   Gi'us a few verses then.

Darren   Eh?

Lucy   Sing us a song. Can just imagine you in one o'them white frocks.

Darren   It's nothin' like that. Oh, gi'oer.

Lucy   You've never shagged 'er 'ave yer?

Pause.

Darren   'Ant seen 'er all week.

Lucy   Not much of a girlfriend then is she?

Darren   Never said it were serious. (*Pause.*) Too posh.

Lucy   What?

Darren   Too posh.

Lucy   Like you, yer mean.

Darren   Naow.

Pause.

Lucy   Why d'yer come?

Darren   'Cause. We're friends, aren't we?

Lucy   Are we?

Darren   Course.

Lucy   What for ever?

Darren   Yeah.

Lucy   For ever and ever and ever?

Darren   I'm 'ere, aren't I?

Long pause.

Lucy   Still somert there, int they? Wunt've bumped into yer otherwise. There is though, int they?

Pause.

Got lovely brown eyes 'ant yer?

Pause.
Lucy *touches* **Darren**, *who clumsily responds.*
They kiss.
Pause.

Darren   They do suit yer, them.

Lucy   What?

Darren   Them trainers. They suit yer.

Lights fade.

Scene Two

A week later. Day.

Lucy, *in her dressing gown, holds the front door open.* **Dave** *is standing in the doorway, carrying a rucksack. Behind him is* **Gonzo**.

Dave   Fuck me, lass, yer deaf or what?

Lucy   You're lookin' well.

Dave   Mind out then.

Dave *and* **Gonzo** *let themselves in,* **Dave** *drops his rucksack by the door.*

Lucy   Caught the sun, 'ant yer?

Dave   Takin' the piss?

Lucy   You 'ave.

Gonzo   Move out, I'm bustin'.

Gonzo *whisks past* **Lucy** *and* **Dave** *and goes through into the bathroom.*

Dave   Yer missed us? 'Ere.

He digs in his jeans pocket and pulls out a small bag of skunk weed.

Bit of a present like. Donkey's knob.

Lucy   Eh?

Dave   That's what they call it. Donkey's knob. Superskunk. Thought yer'd appreciate it.

He hands **Lucy** *the weed.*

Proper potent n'all, so don't go mad.

Lucy   Were just about to run a bath.

Dave   What?

Lucy   Just now.

Dave   'Ant seen yer for over a week.

Lucy   Yeah and I've only just got me giro.

Dave   Aren't yer gonna gi'us a kiss?

He embraces and kisses **Lucy**. *The toilet flushes, offstage.*

Yer missed us? I've missed you.

Lucy   Yer know I 'ave.

Dave *kisses* **Lucy**.

Lucy   There's a funfair just opened in Millhouses.

Dave   Oh. That's nice. So what?

Lucy   There's waltzers n'everythin'. D'yer have a nice time?
Look like yer 'ave.

Dave   Fuckin' see why Anne Frank loved it so much.

Gonzo *re-enters from the toilet, wiping his hands on his jeans.*

Dave   Done a lot o'thinkin', 'ant we Gonz?

Gonzo   Eh?

Dave   Just tellin' Luce 'bout us plans. What we talked
about.

Gonzo   Oh yeah.

Gonzo *sits on the bed and proceeds to build a spliff.*

Dave   I've missed yer, yer know? Med me realise. Not
gettin' any younger are we?

Lucy   No. Eh? What d'yer mean younger?

Dave *runs his fingers through* **Lucy**'s *hair.*

Dave   Little bloody acorn you. 'Ere.

He moves **Lucy** *to the sofa, sits her down next to him.*

Skin one up f'yer if yer like.

He takes the bag of skunk off **Lucy**, *proceeds to build a spliff.*

(*Crap Jamaican accent.*) Bun-up a weed no-gal. T'roat jus' jingle
wi'dat sweet-sweet madda 'erb t'rars.

He laughs at himself.

Fuckin' run out o'money, dint we? 'Ad t'blag it on train back
to Rotterdam in end. On to ferry. Sneakin' through customs
like a pair o'bloody schoolkids, weren't we, Gonz?

Gonzo Jedi mind trick, star.

Dave Yeah, fuckin' . . . Obi-Wan 'ere, gi'in it the old
Crocodile Dundee wi'is fingers. 'Pretend we're invisible,' 'e
sez. Through the barriers, half an ounce wedged under 'is
bollocks, like, fuck me, 'ope yer 'ant got crabs or we'll all be
fucked. Not that we . . . We dint get up to owt or nowt.
Honest, Luce, yer should see 'em, down the red-light district
n'that? Disgustin'. Big fat fuckin' . . . Russians mostly, I
reckon. That or Japs. Fuckin' need a red light to cover up
bruises. (*Pause.*) Sad really. We just stopped round coffee
shops n'that. Bought mesen a T-shirt, look.

*He rolls up his jumper and shows off his 'Bulldog Coffee Shop'
T-shirt.*

Good, innit? Just gettin' mashed like. Talkin'. Med a few
promises dint we Gonz?

Gonzo Yeah. Gonna be good boys from now on.

Dave No more fuckin' shit. Strictly ganja. Start makin' an
effort, innit? I mean, Gonzo's got a family to look after innit?
'Ow d'yer think they must feel? Kid never sees 'is dad no
more.

Gonzo Just get caught up in it all, don't yer? Routine of it.

Dave I mean it, Luce. Look at me.

Lucy What?

Dave 'Ave you even been listenin'?

Lucy 'Course.

Dave   Sat there like a cabbage.

Lucy   You 'ant said nowt.

Dave   F'fucksake . . .

Lucy   You 'ant. Barge in when I'm 'avin' a nice quiet day on me own, I'm a busy woman, Dave. Yer dint even send us a postcard.

Dave   I'm 'ere, aren't I?

Lucy   And what's 'e doin' 'ere? I told yer, I don't want 'im 'ere no more. Looks like a freak wi'that nose. Enough to give yer nightmares.

Dave (*laughs*)   Alright, alright . . .

Lucy   My flat, it's my flat, Dave.

Dave   Yeah, and 'e's a witness int 'e?

Lucy   Eh?

Dave   Stand up. Go on. Stand up.

Lucy   You stand up.

Dave   I'm tryin' to express mesen 'ere.

Lucy   Fine. Never listen to me anyway.

Dave   Look . . . 'Ow can I put this?

Gonzo   Bin doin' a lot o'thinkin'.

Dave   Bin doin' a lot o'thinkin'. 'Bout you n'me, Luce? That's 'alf reason we come back so soon.

Lucy   Thought that's why yer left in first place?

Dave   Yeah and I wanna mek it up to yer, don't I, Gonz?

Gonzo   Can't just run away.

Dave   That's a coward's way out. Honest, Luce, it's opened my eyes out there. Some right scabs. Junkies, fuckin' . . . 'Eadcases innit? I don't wanna end up like that, you don't wanna end up like that, lookin' like that. And I know it's been 'ard on both us, not just me. Fuckin' hate mesen the way I've . . . the way I've . . .

Gonzo   Taken 'er for granted.

Dave   In the past, like, in the past. Not, well . . . Yer know?

Lucy   Slept around.

Dave   Don't put it like that, that's not fair. Alright, it is fair, but that's what I'm sayin', Luce, it's over, I wanna . . . Wanna show yer that I can mek yer happy.

Lucy   I am 'appy.

Dave   No yer not.

Lucy   I am.

Dave   Lucy, you are not happy.

Lucy   But . . .

Dave   Lucy! (*Pause.*) Only 'ave t'look at yer. Look at yer complexion f'fucksake. Too many takeaways that. Need to get a bit o'fruit down yer. Got the diet of a four-year-old, locked in 'ere all day wi'no one to look after yer. Cuts me up just thinkin' of it. Feel like a right fuckin' failure. 'Ere.

He stands and pulls **Lucy** *to her feet.*

Know what's comin', don't yer?

Lucy   Do I?

Dave   What we've always wanted these last six months. 'Ere, Gonz, get the camera, will yer?

Dave *gets down on one knee and digs into his pocket.* **Gonzo** *moves, goes to the rucksack and rummages inside.* **Dave** *pulls a ganja bag out of his pocket, inside is a cheap silver ring. He takes the ring out of the bag.*

Dave   'Ere.

He gives the ring to **Lucy**.

It's not real or owt. Thirty guilders. Stupid really. Always bin a bit of a softie, 'ant I?

Lucy   Since when?

Dave   Since I said, alright? – Don't bend it!

Lucy   I'm not.

Dave   Fucksake, Luce, just put it on, will yer? 'Ere.

Dave *puts the ring on* **Lucy**'s *finger*.

I'm serious, yer know? I'll move in n'everythin'. Get Bill to get us a job on yard again.

Gonzo   Yer sure it's in 'ere?

Dave   Under me keks. Well? 'Ow about it? I will change. Promise. (*Pause.*) Can do it at the weekend if yer like. There's that registry office by the Novotel, yer pass it on bus. That is, if yer want to . . . Yer know? Start a family again.

Lucy   Again?

Dave *dithers, stands.*
Gonzo *finds the camera.*

Dave   Well, not . . . Obviously not again, but . . .

Lucy   Again.

Dave   No, I . . .

Lucy   Like you n'Tanya, yer mean?

Dave   Don't be fuckin' stupid, o'course not, that were . . .

Lucy   Reason she left yer, weren't it?

Dave   Now listen . . .

Lucy   Fuckin' jaffa.

Dave   'Ey!

Lucy   Jaffa. Seedless fuckin' . . .

Dave *strikes* **Lucy**.
Gonzo *takes a picture.*

Dave   Look, just ignore that, alright? (*Pause.*) Luce? Come on, yer know I dint mean it.

Lucy   Bastard.

Dave   Said I'm sorry, dint I?

He gets on his knees again.

(*To Lucy.*) Just slipped out like. Friends? (*Pause.*) Oh come on Luce, don't be a cunt all yer life.

He takes **Lucy**'s *hand.* **Lucy** *pulls away.*

Come on . . .

Lucy   Geddof me!

Gonzo *takes a picture.*

Dave   Gonzo!

Lucy   Two timin' waste o'space.

Lucy *pulls the ring off and throws it across the room.*

Dave   Lucy . . .

Lucy   Fuck off back t'yer barstool!

Lucy *exits into the bathroom.*
Pause.
Taps are heard running, offstage.
Dave *finds the ring.*

Dave (*to Gonzo*)   Don't you say nothin'.

Dave *moves to the bathroom door, knocks.*
Gonzo *sits and finishes building his spliff.*

Dave   'Ere, Luce. Be good though, wunt it? Be good though wunt it, Luce? Make a fresh start. Me dad won't know what's 'it 'im. Be like Madonna n'Guy Ritchie or somert. Posh

n'Becks. Gonz as best man n'that. Show 'em what counts.
Show 'em we can do it.

Lucy *re-enters.*

Lucy   You still 'ere?

Lucy *searches for a towel among the piles of dirty clothes.*

Old enough t'be me father, the state.

Dave   Someone been puttin' ideas into your 'ead? Lucy?
They 'ave, 'ant they?

Lucy   Too much thinkin' does yer brain in anyway.

Dave   What?

Lucy *finds her towel.*

Lucy   Don't look at me like that. Crack'ead. Mongrel. Dirty
fuckin' . . .

Dave *kicks over the television. It smashes.*

Pause.

Lucy   So? That prove yerra man, does it?

Dave   No. No it dunt.

He gathers his belongings.

Pathetic.

Lucy   I know you are.

Dave   Women out there'd love to rip the pants off me, yer
know? Should count yer bloody chickens I stick wi'it. Lucky
I'm so patient. You want time t'think about it, fine, fuckin'
fine. But I'm not gonna be around for ever, Luce. I'm not
Dracula. Yer do realise that, don't yer?

Pause.

Well? Look at me, f'fucksake. I'm talkin', Luce.

Lucy   Yer'll pay f'that n'all. Yer will.

Pause.
Dave *tries to hug* **Lucy**, *who backs off.*

Lucy   Fuck off, will . . . ?!

Dave   Listen!

Lucy   No!

Dave   I forgive yer, alright? I forgive yer. (*Pause.*) 'Ere.

He digs in his pocket, pulls out a couple of notes – two fivers.

All I've got.

He gives **Lucy** *the notes.*

Treat yersen. On me, yeah? Get a pizza or somert.

Lucy *stuffs the notes in her mouth, chews them up and spits them out.* **Dave** *gathers the wet notes off the floor.*

Dave   Look . . . Look, just gi'us a call, yeah?

He takes his rucksack, moves to the door.

When yer ready.

Lucy   I've already told yer, Dave, I'm . . .

Dave   When yer ready, I said. Well?

Lucy *blows a raspberry.*

Dave   'Bout time you grew up, Luce.

Lucy   Would do if yer'd fuck off stalkin' me.

Dave   I will.

Lucy   Go on then.

Dave   I will.

Lucy   Run back to Daddy.

Dave   There's no turnin' back, yer know?

Lucy   Good.

Dave   This is it, Luce. Once I step out that door.

Lucy   Honest?

Dave   On the fuckin' cross, yeah.

Lucy   Can I 'ave that in writin'?

Dave   Yer gonna call us or what?

Lucy   Call you a cunt. Useless.

Dave   You are. Yer fuckin' are, Luce.

Lucy   Need a real man, me.

Dave   Oh yeah?

Lucy   Yeah. Someone 'oo dunt cream all over sheets before we've even started. True though, int it?

Dave   Slut.

Lucy   That's me alright.

Dave   Yer'll see.

Lucy   Mel bloody B!

Dave   Don't know what's good f'yer!

Dave *exits, slamming the door.*
Pause.

Gonzo   Told 'im yer weren't worth it.

Lucy   You can get lost n'all. Bloody choke chain. Well, go on.

Gonzo *rests himself and lights his spliff.*
Lucy *goes to the television and puts it back in place.*
Long pause.
Darren, *in just his boxer shorts, crawls out from under the bed.*

Lucy   You alright? D'yer wanna cuppa?

Gonzo   'Ere, that's some bloody bedbug, Luce.

Lucy   See what I 'ave to put up with?

Gonzo   Should ring the council 'bout that.

Lucy   'Oo asked you?

Blackout.

Scene Three

A month later. Evening.

Lucy *and* **Nikki** *and* **Jo** *sit, drinking glasses of cheap wine, smoking. Plate of biscuits on the table. New second-hand television.*

Nikki   Can't believe it, can you?

Jo   No, God 'elp us.

Nikki   When d'yer find out?

Lucy   Last week.

Nikki   Arrr. Can't believe it.

Jo   Oh for . . . Would you cut it out?

Nikki   What?

Lucy *nudges* **Nikki**.

Lucy   Can't believe it meself, Nik.

Nikki   Me neither. Thought of any names yet?

Lucy   Fucksake, Nikki, gi'us a chance.

Nikki   I like Fred me.

Lucy   Fred?

Nikki   What's wrong wi'Fred? It's different innit. Fred forra boy, Rose forra girl. Fred and Rosemary West, geddit?

Jo *scowls at* **Nikki**.

Nikki   I'm jokin'.

Lucy   Might not call it owt. Just call it. (*Pulls a face.*)

Nikki   Eh?

Lucy   Well it's different innit.

Nikki   Won't get very far with a name like – (*Pulls a face.*) 'Ow's 'e gonna know when it's 'is teatime.

Lucy   Put it on table, won't I? 'E'll smell it.

Nikki   More like a dog than a kid.

Lucy   Tek after 'is dad then, won't 'e?

Nikki   Mus' be made up.

Lucy   Yeah. Yeah I am.

Nikki   I think it's fab.

Jo   Jesus Christ.

Lucy   Oh, cheer up, Gran, it's not the end o'the world.

Jo   Yer said that last time.

Lucy   That were last time. Besides, I'm still 'ere, aren't I?

Jo   Just about.

Nikki   Oh, come on, it's not every day yer find out yer gonna be a great-grandmother.

Lucy   She'll come round.

Jo   S'ppose I'll 'ave to when yer run out o'bloody food.

Nikki   Oh, 'ave a biscuit n'shut up.

Lucy   Miserable old git.

Jo   'Ant you got a conscience? Thought yer'd've learnt yer lesson be now. Look. Look at it.

She points to the framed picture of the baby.

She's not dead, yer know?

Nikki   Gran!

Lucy   No, but she might as bloody well be.

Nikki   Be alright t'come n'babysit, won't it?

Lucy   'Course. Once we're settled.

Nikki   I'm great wi'kids me.

Lucy   'Ope yer both hungry. Get an Indian in a bit. I'll send Darren on an errand.

Jo   Oh, so 'e's got a name 'as 'e?

Lucy   'E's movin' in next week.

Nikki   Arrr. Who's Darren?

Lucy   Who d'yer think?

Nikki   But . . . What 'appened t'Dave?

Lucy   Kicked the telly over.

Nikki   Oh. Oh! That's nice! Little portable, look.

Lucy   Darren brought it over from 'is on New Year. Same night we conceived like.

Nikki   Now how romantic is that.

Jo   Please.

Nikki   And t'think I was sat in wi'old misery guts 'ere.

Jo   What d'yer mean? We 'ad a lovely night.

Nikki   Yeah, right. Two words, Luce. Freddie bloody Mercury.

Lucy   Oh, Gran.

Nikki   Wish I'd never bought 'er that Queen video now. Never 'ear the end of it.

Jo   Man's a legend.

Nikki   I don't care.

Jo   Man's a legend, Nikki.

Lucy   Least yer dint 'ave the whole estate barkin' on till four in the mornin'. Drove me up the wall.

Nikki   Can't stop people enjoyin' 'emselves, Luce.

Lucy   It's not that I've got a problem with. It's all that Happy New Year's shite I can't stand. Fuckin' stupid. Me n'Darren sat in, right? All cosy on sofa there. Suddenly, stroke o'midnight, ding bloody dong. Fireworks on telly n'that. Did me 'ead right in it did. All oer estate like. Runnin' out o'flats like mice and on to balconies. All the families givin' it whatsit. 'Old Land's Eye' n'that. Drownin' out the flat like a bunch o'bloody moggies. N'I'm like, what? Like we're all suddenly best mates or somert. I mean, every other day o'the year, it's fuck you, don't wanna know yer. Fuck you, out the way. But suddenly, turn o'century and it's like, yeah, let's 'ave a bloody singalong. Pat each other on the back and for what? So they can turn round next day and stab yer in the back? Dunt mek sense. Even 'ad to stop Darren joinin' in at one point.

Pause.

Nikki   Least yer conceived though, eh?

Lucy   We were dancin' all night.

Nikki   And the rest.

Lucy (*giggles*)   Yeah, well . . .

Nikki   Arrr, look at 'er, she's blushin', look.

Lucy   'E bought us flowers n'everythin'. Breakfast in bed.

Nikki   Arrr.

Lucy   He's got a job n'that. Renovations.

Nikki   I think it's dead sweet me. Wish Brendan was that thoughtful.

Jo (*to* **Lucy**)   See what yer've done? Puttin' ideas in 'er 'ead.

Lucy   Takes two to tango, Gran. Learnt that off me mum. Look at us two, f'fucksake. 'Ardly the bloody Brady Bunch, are we?

Jo   That's not fair, Lucy.

Lucy   Well. Don't 'ear me complainin'.

Nikki   Lucky if I can drag 'im off that bloody PlayStation, never mind no tango.

Lucy   Wunt stand for'it me.

Nikki   Should see 'is thumbs. Blisters all oer the ends there.

Lucy   Should chop 'em off.

Nikki   N'go out wi'some spastic? You're weird.

Lucy   Don't knock it. Know where yer stand wi' disabled. Know where their loyalties lie, for one. Long as yer make 'em feel human.

Nikki   What? And 'ave 'em wrigglin' under the covers 'cause they can't keep still?

Lucy   Why not?

Nikki   'Ave yer not seen 'em on the telly? Can't even talk right.

Lucy   Show us a bloke 'oo can.

Nikki   True. (*Pause.*) Cunt share same bed though still. Might start bitin' yer or somert. Dribblin' on yer shoulder – Uurgh.

Jo   Should 'ave you two lobotomised, talkin' like that. Disgustin'.

Nikki   Oh, 'ere she goes.

Jo   'Ant yer got no manners? They can't 'elp the way they look, poor sods.

Lucy   Never said they were poor.

Jo Yer know what I mean, Lucy.

Lucy Just statin' a fact. Yer know where you are wi'disabled. What's wrong wi'that? It's you who's turnin' 'em into some sort o'special case, Gran.

Nikki Dunno if 'e even wants kids. Brendan, I mean. Never asked.

Lucy What's to ask? Just gotta take a few days off, 'ant yer? 'E'll never know.

Nikki What? Yer mean . . . ? No, I couldn't.

Jo You leave 'er out o'this.

Lucy She's gotta mind of 'er own.

Jo Not with you around she 'ant.

Nikki 'Ey, d'yer mind?

Lucy Pay no attention, Nik.

Nikki Do what I want. My life.

Jo Yes and if yer'd got any sense yer'd get yerself to college and learn somert before you end up like 'er.

Lucy She's not an idiot, Gran.

Jo Did you even look at that prospectus I got yer?

Nikki Yeah.

Lucy Give 'er a break, she's only just out o'school.

Jo Only just. 'Ad to bend over backwards just to get 'er in the bloody exam 'all. And no, she's not an idiot. Four GCSEs she got in the end. Proud o'yer n'all, Nikki. F'Godsake, don't waste it.

Nikki I'm not.

Lucy Let 'er live a bit first, will yer?

Jo That's what I'm tryin' to do, Lucy.

Lucy By sendin' 'er to some poncey college wi'a bunch o'bloody lah-di-dah students.

Jo There's countries'd kill for an education system like ours, Lucy. D'yer ever watch the news? There's kids your age in Africa don't even 'ave runnin' water never mind no . . .

Lucy Let 'em fuckin' 'ave it then. Rather starve.

Jo Just a bloody game to you, isn't it?

Lucy I never learnt owt.

Jo Yer never even tried.

Lucy Yes I did, I were in top classes for ages.

Jo You were sleepin' with yer bloody form tutor!

Nikki Oh, come on, Gran, we've only just got 'ere.

Jo Yes and I'm sick t'the stomach already.

Nikki Give 'er a chance.

Jo No-good bloody . . .

She grabs her bag and coat.

Never learn, d'yer?

Lucy Must be genetic then innit?

Jo You need to learn some self-respect, girl. What d'yer think's gonna happen after that one drops?

Lucy Nothin'.

Jo Exactly. Nothin'. Wait till me or its dad or the bloody social come and tek it away, while yer . . . sit there and wait f'some other walkin' sperm bank come knockin' on the door. 'Ave you even 'ad a check-up?

Lucy What?

Jo AIDS, darlin', AIDS.

Lucy   Cross that bridge when I come to it, won't I?

Nikki   Lucy.

Lucy   Don't you start n'all.

Nikki   Gotta be careful now, yer know? Never know who yer might . . .

Jo   'Course she's not bloody careful, look at 'er. Does 'e even know? This Dazwell.

Lucy   Darren.

Jo   Whatever. Yer sure it's even his?

Lucy   I'm not a slut, Gran.

Nikki   She's not.

Jo   Oh, shuddup, Nikki.

Nikki   Gran!

Lucy   Should be dead and buried be now anyway.

Nikki   'Ey! Don't say that.

Jo (*to* **Nikki**)   Come on. Get yer things together.

She pulls a Walkman out of her handbag and proceeds to put it on.

Can't believe I missed *Watchdog* f'this.

Jo, *with Walkman, exits through the alcove into the bathroom.*

Lucy   Should o'bloody poisoned yer!

Pause.

Nikki   Don't worry, she'll be alright in a minute. Life-saver that Walkman.

Pause.

Shunt o'said that, Luce. Yer know she's not bin well.

Lucy   Thought yer'd be pleased.

Nikki   'Course she's pleased, Luce, we both are. She's just old, yer know? Wunt even go n'cash 'er pension other day. 'Ad to do it for 'er while she sits at 'ome with 'er feet up. Like she's given up.

Pause.

Lucy   It is different. This time.

Nikki   Yer gonna get married?

Lucy   Dunno.

Nikki   Best thing in the world aren't they? Babies. Way the little faces scrunch up n'that. Don't know nothin' d'they? What they've got comin' to 'em n'that.

Lucy   I like their 'ands.

Pause.

Nikki   Wish yer'd come back 'ome.

Lucy   Eh?

Nikki   Wish yer'd . . .

Darren *enters through the front door.*

Lucy   Oh, 'ello!

Darren (*to* **Lucy**)   I need to talk t'yer.

Nikki   Is that 'im?

She gets up and hugs **Darren**.

Arrr, look at 'im. 'E's just a kid 'imself!

Lucy   I know.

Nikki   Like a tweenie.

Lucy   I know.

Nikki   It is Darren, yeah? 'Ey, congratulations . . .

Darren   Yeah . . .

Nikki   Lucy were just tellin' us.

Darren   Look, Luce . . .

Nikki   I'm Nikki, by the way.

Lucy   Don't be ignorant, Darren.

Darren   Pleased t'meet yer. Could I just . . .

Nikki   Lucy's told us all about yer.

Darren *moves past* **Nikki** *and goes to* **Lucy**.

Lucy   'Ad a good day?

Darren   Can we talk?

Lucy   'Course we can. Must be exhausted.

Nikki   'Ere, Gran! Darren's 'ere!

Darren   In private.

Lucy   This is private.

Nikki *knocks on the bathroom door.*

Nikki   Gran!

Darren   I need to . . .

Lucy   Don't I get a kiss on the cheek?

Nikki   'Urry up!

Darren   Look . . .

Lucy   Kiss please.

Darren *hesitates, then kisses* **Lucy** *on the cheek.*

Lucy   Thought we'd get an Indian in a bit.

Darren   Fucksake, listen to me, will yer?!

Nikki   Gran! What yer doin' in there?

Jo *enters from the bathroom, taking off her Walkman.*

Jo   What d'yer think I'm bloody – Oh, 'ello, duck.

Darren   Sorry, I dint mean to snap, it's just . . .

Nikki   Let's stay forra bit, eh? Come on.

Darren   Can we talk?

Jo   It's Darren, isn't it?

Nikki   That's our Gran.

Jo   I'm not a waxwork, Nikki. Name's Joan. Jo for short.

Darren *reluctantly shakes hands.*

Darren   Nice to meet yer.

Jo   Little sweetie, aren't yer?

Lucy   Don't be rude, Darren.

Jo   I hear yer in renovations.

Darren   Yeah. Family thing.

Lucy   Proper little businessman.

Jo   Really?

Nikki   Don't 'og 'im, Gran.

Jo   What yer doin' wi'this one then?

Nikki   Gran!

Jo   She payin' yer?

Darren   I'm not.

Jo   Sorry?

Darren   I'm not with anyone, alright? Lucy, please.

Lucy   Well, come on, sit down everyone, sit down.

Jo, **Nikki**, **Darren** and **Lucy** *sit down.*
Lucy *picks a selection of takeaway pamphlets.*

Lucy   Right. What would everyone like? They all deliver.
Golden Poppadum does a really nice korma, but it is a bit
dear. Could just 'ave a pizza, if yer like. Domino's do a family

meal, look. Chicken wings, garlic bread, bottle o'Coke. Well? Darren?

Darren   I'm not 'ungry.

Lucy   'Course you are. We're celebratin', aren't we? Well?

Pause.

Nikki   Lovely eyes.

Lucy   And teeth look.

Pause.

Jo   Yer sure this is 'im?

Nikki   Could just get some chips, cunt we? D'yer fancy chips, Luce?

Lucy   Was there somert yer wanted to tell me? Darren!

Darren   It's kind o'private, alright?

Lucy   Oh, don't worry 'bout these two. Lips are sealed, aren't they, girls?

Darren   This int a bloody joke, Luce.

Lucy   Who's jokin'?

Nikki   Look, maybe we should . . .

Lucy   Oh no yer don't.

Jo   Poor lad doesn't know what 'e's got 'imself in for.

Lucy   D'yer mind?

Jo   Yer not the first one either, son.

Lucy   'Ere, shall we make a toast, Nik?

Nikki   Eh?

Lucy   Raise yer glasses then. Come on. Come on.

She raises her glass, as do **Nikki** *and* **Jo**, *reluctantly.*

Don't be a gooseberry, Darren, join in.

Nikki   'E 'ant got nowt.

Lucy   Well 'e'll just 'ave to pretend, won't yer? Go on. (*Pause.*) Darren. Darren! Raise yer bloody glass! Now!

Darren *raises his hand, as though holding a glass.*

Lucy   The future.

Nikki/Jo/Darren (*mumbled*)   The future.

They drink.
Long pause.

Nikki   So. Renovations, yeah?

Lucy   Shall we just skip the main course? Don't move, alright?

Lucy *exits into the kitchen.*

Nikki   Nice of yer to bring yer telly over.

Darren   What?

Nikki   The telly there. Really nice.

Darren   Don't know what you're talkin' about, sorry.

Nikki   Must be dead excited.

Jo   It'll all end in tears, yer know?

Lucy *re-enters, with a cake on a plate and a carving knife. The cake is lopsided, stuffed with cream – a mess.*

Lucy   'Ere we are. Enough for everyone, look.

She sits, placing the cake down before them all.

Good, int it? Less personal when yer buy it from shop.

She cuts the cake into four quarters.

Don't mind eatin' with yer hands, do yer?

She hands the pieces out to **Nikki**, **Jo** *and* **Darren**.

Nikki   Is that . . . ? It is n'all. Lucy.

Lucy   What?

Nikki   There's egg yolk in this. You 'ant mixed it right.

Lucy   Yes I 'ave.

Jo   Yer can't be serious, Lucy. Lucy.

Lucy   Yer'll eat it won't yer, Darren?

Jo   And die of bloody food poisoning.

Lucy   'Course yer will.

Nikki   Uuuuur.

Lucy   Come on, Darren.

Nikki   Yer smelt it?

Jo   Don't shove it in my facc, Nikki, I'm . . .

Darren   Oh, f'fucksake!

Darren *throws his piece of cake down.*

Lucy   Darren!

Darren *moves to the front door, opens it.*

Lucy   Darren!

Darren (*to* **Jo** *and* **Nikki**)   Please. Could yer please just . . . ?

Lucy   Don't you make a fuckin' fool o'me . . .

Darren   I don't know what she told . . .

Lucy   I'm warnin' yer, yer little . . .

Darren   Fuck you, alright? Fuck you, fuck yer cake, fuck yer whole fuckin' family, alright?!

Lucy *slams her piece of cake into* **Darren**'s *face.*
Long pause.

Darren (*to* **Nikki** *and* **Jo**)   If yer don't mind.

Lucy *takes the last slice of cake and starts eating.*

Jo *and* **Nikki** *gather their things together.*

Lucy   Yeah, that's right, take 'is side why not.

Nikki (*to* **Lucy**)   Yer gonna be alright? Give us a ring, yeah?

Lucy *is eating.*

Nikki   Luce?

Jo   Come on, love, come on.

Nikki *and* **Jo** *head towards the exit.* **Jo** *whispers in* **Darren**'s *ear.*
Nikki *and* **Jo** *exit.* **Darren** *shuts the door behind them.* **Darren**
wipes the cake from his face.
Long pause.

Darren   Don't believe you.

Lucy   Yeah, well, someone's gotta make an effort, 'ant they?
Where were yer anyway? Said yer'd be 'ere by seven.

Darren   I'm sick o'this, Luce.

Lucy   Yeah and I'm sick o'waitin'.

Darren   Phone ringin' every 'alf-hour . . .

Lucy   What d'yer expect?

Darren   I thought I'd med meself clear. I'm not interested.
A man makes a mistake, alright? (*Pause.*) Just one o'them
things. (*Pause.*) An accident, f'fucksake, that's all it were, a
stupid accident. (*Pause.*) Long as we face up t'the facts, show a
bit o'maturity. I mean . . . (*Pause.*) Nob'dy's to know, are they?

Pause.
*He digs into his pocket and pulls out a piece of paper with a phone
number on it.*

Look. 'Av got the number o'this clinic. 'Ere.

He hands the paper to **Lucy**.

Up Nether Edge? I'll pay for it. Use me savin's n'that.

Lucy *examines the paper.*

Darren   Go there in the mornin', if yer like. I'll tek the day off 'specially.

Pause.

This int easy for me either, yer know?

Pause.

Tell yer what. (*Pause.*) I'll just go n'mek us both a drink, yeah? (*Pause.*) While yer think about it.

He exits into the kitchen.
Pause.
Lucy *puts the piece of paper down, stands.*

Darren (*off*)   Yer got any milk?

Lucy *takes the carving knife and moves to the kitchen.*

Darren (*off*)   Lucy?

Lucy *exits into the kitchen.*
Pause.

Darren (*off*)   Aaaahh! Fuckin' 'ell! Fuckin'! Aaaah!

Lucy *re-enters, goes to the chest of drawers, picks up the picture of the baby. She sits. Stands the picture. She wipes her eyes and lights a fag.*
Darren *re-enters, his fingers are cut and badly bleeding.*

Darren   Fuckin' . . .

Darren *exits into the bathroom.*
Lucy *moves the TV, starts flicking through the channels.*
Darren *re-enters, wrapping toilet roll round his blood-sodden hand.*

Darren   Don't 'ave t'take this, yer know?

Lucy   Gotta learn some'ow.

Darren *sits on the bed, nurses his hand.*

Darren   What's wrong with yer?

Lucy   Nowt. What's wrong with you?

Pause.

Anyway. Not the first time yer've cut yerself, is it?

Long pause.
Lucy *stands, moves over to* **Darren**, *who is in agony. She sits by* **Darren**.

Darren   F'Chrissakes, Luce . . .

Lucy   Actin' all the big man.

Darren   It's just . . .

Lucy   Yer drippin' all over the lino. 'Ere.

Lucy *delicately takes* **Darren**'s *blood-sodden hand.*

Darren   Yer know I don't mean nothin' by it don't yer?

She slowly removes the toilet paper.

Lucy   Just get scared sometimes.

Lucy *slowly licks the wounds clean.*
Pause.

There. That's better. Shall we start again?

Darren   I can't do it, Luce.

Lucy   Darren . . .

Darren   I can't.

Lucy   We're not murderers f'fucksake.

Darren   Well yer 'ant exactly med it easy for me, 'ave yer? (*Pause.*) Sorry.

Lucy   You walked out on me, remember?

Darren   I know.

Lucy   I know yer know.

Pause.

Darren   Shunt've even bin 'ere.

Lucy   So none of it meant nothin' no?

Darren   No. I mean, yes, 'course it did, yer know it did. It's just . . . It's just . . .

Lucy   What?

Darren   There's choices int there?

Lucy   Choices.

Darren   Choices.

Lucy   Right and wrong, yeah?

Darren   Don't do this t'me, Luce.

Lucy   D'yer believe in Hell?

Darren   Yeah. 'Course I bloody do.

Lucy   Scares the shit out o'me. 'Ere, see what me sister brought us.

Lucy *finds Cluedo.*

Still got all the pieces I think.

Lucy *sits with Cluedo.*
She opens the box.
Pause as she checks for the pieces.

Lucy   Takes yer back dunt it?

Darren   Too young f'this.

Lucy   Yer told yer dad yet?

Darren   Eh?

Lucy   'Bout us, yer told 'im 'bout us? Well?

Pause.

Ooh, look. It's the dog from Monopoly, look. What's 'e doin' in there?

Darren   I can't.

Lucy   What?

Darren   I can't. 'E'd go mad, Luce.

Darren *sits back on the bed, while* **Lucy** *looks through Cluedo.* **Darren** *begins to cry.*

Lucy   'Ant seen yer in days, thought yer might . . .

Darren   Yer don't know what 'e's like. If 'e knew . . .

Lucy   It's Karen int it? Darren. She been puttin' ideas in your 'ead?

Darren   No.

Lucy   She 'as, 'ant she?

Darren   It's nowt to do with 'er.

Lucy   What is it then?

Darren   All of 'em. If they knew, if they even knew I was 'ere . . .

Lucy   Oh, baby. Don't cry. Don't cry.

Darren   Jus' me dad . . .

Lucy *hugs* **Darren**.

Lucy   Come on. (*Pause.*) Can't just stick it in the shit can we? What'll 'e think? (*Pause.*) I mean, yer do believe don't yer?

Darren   Eh?

Lucy   'E died for our sins, Darren. 'E did.

Darren   I know.

Lucy   Tell yer what, I'll even come along if yer want. Church I mean. (*Pause.*) Proper little choir girl me, yer know? Could show that Karen a thing or two. (*Sings.*) 'Kum by yah, me lord, Kum by yah.' Should 'ear my Amazin' Grace. Bin known t'shatter milk floats that.

Darren *stifles a laugh.*

Lucy   That's better.

Lucy *wipes* **Darren***'s face with her sleeve.*

Lucy   See? Dunt matter really.

She moves. She lights a candle by the bed and turns the light off. The only light in the room comes from the candle and the television.

That's better, int it? Sleep better now, can't we?

She kisses **Darren***.*

Gonna be beautiful.

Darren   Yeah?

Lucy   Yeah.

She kisses **Darren***, holding him tight.*
Pause.

Fuckin' beautiful.

Darren   Yeah.

Lucy   This is it now.

Darren   I know.

Lucy   Yer'll see.

She pulls **Darren***'s head on to her lap, stroking him.*

All make sense in the end. You n'me. Our own little home. Do it up a bit, like. Lick o'paint. Put a throw over that thing. Frame on picture there. Love that picture. Sez somethin', dunt it? Really somert special about that. Only ever notice it when I'm . . . (*Pause.*) Be able to decorate won't we? Once we're settled. Nice blue carpet. Blue or green at any rate, long as it's furry. Able to walk barefoot then. Barefoot in us dressin' gowns. Couple o'lamps. Bookshelf. Sofa. Coffee-table. Spiderplant. Video. Hoover. Keep it all clean. Washin' machine. Go Kwik Save on Sunday. Economise. (*Pause.*) *Radio Times.* Jus' bein' 'ere. Together. You comin' back from work, n'avin' a shower. Nice cold shower. Don't even 'ave to say

owt if yer don't want, dunt bother me. Prefer it that way.
Long as we both know. Long as it dunt turn into owt. Jus'
sittin' 'ere. Thinkin'. Lick o'paint on the walls. Be lovely.
(*Long pause.*) And Christmas. (*Long pause.*) Stay in bed at
weekends. Snuggled up like Teddy bears. Won't even answer
door. Nowt t'prove anymore. Long as we both know. Long as
we both know.

Lights fade.

Scene Four

Three months later. Morning.

*The flat is much the same, only messier. Two tins of yellow paint are
stacked by the wall, near the window. One of them is opened. By the tins
is a rollerbrush, smothered with dry crusty yellow paint, and a dirty
black palatte. On the wall is a small patch of yellow paint, the start of a
failed job.*

Dave *and* **Gonzo** *sit together.* **Gonzo** *is preparing a crackpipe.*

Lucy *can be heard vomiting from the bathroom.*

Dave   Fuck me, 'av you 'eard it? Fuckin' Bride
o'Chewbacca in there. Bin like this f'days now.

Gonzo   She alright?

Dave   'Ant said owt.

Gonzo   Wunt worry about it, star. Our Jocy were same
when she were flyin' flag. Fuckin' pukin', shits, spinnin' out
like a fuckin' whizzed-up mongol. Distressin's not the word,
star. Whoooo! 'Ad to . . . yer know? Sort 'er out, like. Yer
know? Just t'save me bacon, like. Woman 'ad one o'them
whatsits? Kitchen utensil.

Dave   What, like a slotted spoon?

Gonzo   No, more like a whatsit skewer f'carvin' up yer joint
like? Forked prongs n'shit, this close to me heart.

Dave   Fuck.

Gonzo   This close, star. I mean . . . Somert missin' there, int they?

Dave   Yeah.

Gonzo   Somert missin' there, like . . . Fuck off, yer know? Grown woman. Tellin' yer. Not easy bein' a man.

Dave   Not in this day n'age.

Gonzo   Not easy bein' a man.

Dave   That's what me dad said. Over the moon 'e is. Thought 'e were gonna pop 'is clogs when I told 'im.

Gonzo   Another one in fold.

Dave   Long bloody last.

Gonzo   All about bloodline though int it?

Dave   All we've got in end.

Gonzo   Mystery o'creation, star.

Dave   Big bang.

Gonzo   Somert like that.

Dave   Big fuckin' bang, eh Gonz?

They laugh.

Gonzo   'Ere, pass us that pin there. Tight as me sister's fuckin' chaff this.

Dave *passes the pin to* **Gonzo**, *who prepares the crackpipe.*

Gonzo   Yep. Nowt like a baby t'send yer fuckin' west. Why d'yer think I'm such an insomniac? Like a bloody owl these days. Be growin' fuckin' feathers next.

Dave   Can't bloody wait, Gonz. Bin tryin' ages f'this.

Gonzo   You n'Luce like?

Dave   No me n'yer mum, Gonz, 'course me n'Luce.

Pause.

Thought I wa' . . . Yer know? Forra bit.

Gonzo   What, like . . . ?

Dave   Yeah. Don't tell no one though.

Gonzo   'Course.

Dave   'Ad a bust-up over it n'all. Well, you were there, weren't yer?

Gonzo   Reckon she wa' already gone?

Dave   Just before the 'oliday, like, yeah.

Gonzo   That explains it then. Fuckin' nervous system goes AWOL, dunt it? Fragile breed, star.

Dave   Get all 'et up over nowt. I mean, tek Luce there. Fuckin' needs an 'ug once in a while, yer know? Just t'soften 'er up. Very sensitive nature. Born t'be a mother like. I mean, she's already got one daughter. Fuckin' nob'ead teacher, right? English teacher when she were at school like. Raped 'er. Lost 'is job n'everythin'. 'Ad to move in 'ere. 'Im n'Luce like . . . Like Michael Douglas n'that. Sick. She were only fifteen at time.

Gonzo   Guy needs a slap.

Dave   That's where I come in, innit? Once 'e fucked off back to 'is wife. Lucy left on 'er tod wi'baby, I mean . . . Yer don't do that do yer?

Gonzo   'Ere.

Gonzo *passes* **Dave** *the crackpipe and the lighter.*

Dave   'Ad t'show 'im what's what.

Gonzo   Flattened 'im, yeah?

Dave   Smashed 'is windows dint I? Put a beer glass on 'is doorstep. 'Ad shit in it like.

Gonzo   Like it, star, like it.

Dave *lights and smokes the rock.* **Gonzo** *lights two cigarettes, smokes one, lets the other burn.* **Lucy** *enters from the bathroom in a long T-shirt. She looks awful. She goes to bed and tries to sleep.*

Long pause as **Dave** *and* **Gonzo** *smoke.*

Gonzo   *Big Breakfast'*ll be on soon.

Long pause.

Dave   Not the same wi'out Denise Van Outen.

Gonzo   Kelly Brook were good though.

Long pause.

Dave   Should put some music on.

Long pause.

Gonzo   What 'appened?

Dave   There's tapes in that box there.

Gonzo   No. T'the baby n'that.

Dave   Oh. Fuckin' social warnt it? Last year.

Long pause.
Gonzo *starts loading up another pipe.*

Gonzo   Start again though now, can't yer?

Dave   Due in September like. Start movin' me stuff in.

Gonzo   Do it up a bit, yeah?

Dave   Don't remind me.

He signals out the paint pots.

Went schiz on me the other day. Only bought 'em to keep 'er 'appy and I told 'er, 'I'm not 'avin' you breathin' in a load o'fuckin' paint fumes.' Poor little thing'll be trippin' 'is nuts off wi'that lot on the walls. I mean, I will do it, but, yer know? Now's not the time is it? It's baby comes first. That's all that matters. Good clean birth, no messin'. (*Pause.*) Take 'em down park wi'football.

Gonzo   'Oo's that then?

Dave   Little un like. Bit o'togger. Swimmin' baths. I'm not 'avin' 'im bein' no fat fuck. Gotta fend f'yersen these days. Cruel fuckin' world out there.

Gonzo   Should take 'em boxin'.

Dave   Get a punchbag hooked up, yeah. Set o'gloves.

Gonzo   What if it's a girl?

Dave   Eh?

Gonzo   Never know.

Dave   She can get a fuckin' education then, can't she?

Pause.

Anyway.

He wrenches himself up and moves to the cassette recorder and the box of tapes. Starts looking through them.

F'fucksake, Luce.

Gonzo   What?

Dave   Bob Marley all the fuckin' time.

Gonzo   Need a bit o'bass line, star. 'Ant she got no 'ouse?

Dave   Lucky if I find a fuckin' kennel in this lot.

Gonzo *starts mixing the cigarette ash in the crack bowl.*

Dave   Simon n'Garfunkel.

Gonzo   'Oo?

Dave (*laughs*)   Simon n'Garfunkel, mate.

Gonzo (*laughs*)   Yer takin' the piss?

Dave   That's all she's got.

He puts on the tape, presses play. He moves back next to **Gonzo***, sits. 'Bridge over Troubled Water' comes on.* **Dave** *and* **Gonzo** *sit in*

*silence for a few moments as the music plays. Then they burst out
laughing.*

Dave   It's not mine!

Lucy *stirs.*

Lucy   Dave.

The laughing continues.

Dave.

The laughing continues.
She sits up in bed, crying.

Dave, please!

The laughing continues.
She rushes to the tape-recorder, switches it off, takes the tape out.

Yer know it makes me cry, it always makes me cry.

The laughing continues.
Lucy *goes back to bed.*
The laughter subsides.

Dave   Fucksake, Luce, we were listenin' t'that!

Pause.

Luce! . . . Lucy! 'Ey!

Dave *gets up, moves over to the bed.*
Gonzo *continues mixing the ash with the rock, subsequently smoking it
as the dialogue continues.*

Dave   Lucy.

He shakes **Lucy.**

'Ey.

Lucy (*from under the covers*)   What yer 'ave t'do that for? Yer
know what it does t'me.

Dave   Oh, come on, Luce, it's only a song. 'Ere.

He sits on the bed and lifts **Lucy** *up, who is clutching the cassette, tears in her eyes.*

(*Laughs.*) Need a bloody crane f'yer soon, won't we? Come on now.

He takes the cassette from her.

Lucy   Can't sleep.

Dave   What?

Lucy   Can't sleep wi'your. Noisy bastards.

Dave   Don't be like that.

Dave *stands, lifts* **Lucy** *off the bed.*

Lucy   Dave.

Dave   Come on. I wanna show Gonz.

Lucy   I'm tired.

Dave   Thought yer cunt sleep.

Lucy   I can't.

Dave   Well then.

He escorts **Lucy** *and seats her between him and* **Gonzo**. **Gonzo** *smoking the pipe.*

Dave   See? Better already.

Lucy *grabs an Argos catalogue.*

Lucy   S'pposed t'be goin' shoppin' today.

Dave   Yeah. Gonzo's gonna drive us, aren't yer?

Gonzo   What?

Lucy   'Elp me decide then.

Dave   I am.

Lucy   S'pposed to be a family now.

Dave We are, Luce. Why d'yer think I – 'Ere save a bit f'me, yer fuck.

Gonzo Only jus' sparked it.

Dave Fuck off, will yer?

Gonzo Yeah, n'there's still . . .

Dave Put it down.

Gonzo . . . two bits there . . .

Dave Gonzo.

Gonzo It's fuckin' dust, look.

Dave 'Ey!

Gonzo (*puts pipe down*) Dust.

Dave I know what yer like, mate.

He grabs the pipe and the lighter, sparks up the pipe. **Lucy** *is flicking through the Argos catalogue.*

Dave Oh look, there's fuck-all there.

Gonzo I told yer it's dust.

Dave Where? I don't see no dust. Just fuckin' foil, look. Dead.

Gonzo Alright, I'll load one up then.

Dave Cheap scammin' twat.

Gonzo Fucksake, Dave.

Dave You 'ant 'idden none, 'ave yer? There were three there a minute ago.

Gonzo What d'yer think that was?

Dave What?

Gonzo Just then. Before.

Dave There were three there, Gonz.

Gonzo   Yeah, three includin' the one we just . . .

Dave   Bollocks, mate. One, two, three. There were three.

Gonzo *starts loading up the pipe.* **Dave** *starts searching round the floor.*

Dave   Fuck this. I know what I saw.

Gonzo   Wastin' yer time, star.

Dave   Fuckin' . . . I saw it, mate. Just . . .

Pause as he searches.

. . . two seconds ago.

Gonzo (*laughs*)   Dave, mate, there int nothin' there.

Dave *gets up off the floor.*

Dave   Yer dint pick it up, did yer?

Gonzo   Eh?

Dave *leans over* **Lucy** *and rummages through* **Gonzo**'s *shirt pocket.*

Gonzo   Dave!

Dave   Yer did, dint yer? Probably shoved it up yer big fuckin' beak there, innit? Come on . . .

Gonzo   What?

Dave   On yer feet, come on.

Gonzo   F'fucksake, 'ere!

He stands, pulls a rock, wrapped in a Rizla, from his jeans pocket.

'Appy now?

Gonzo *sits and gives the rock to* **Dave**.
Dave *unwraps the rock, checks it.*

Dave   Fuckin' slippery little cunt, you, aren't yer? Go on then, rack it up.

Gonzo   Yeah, well, if yer'd stop fuckin' frettin' forra minute.

Pause.
He starts loading up the pipe.

Last time though, yeah?

Dave   'Course. First proper binge in ages this.

Gonzo   Guess it dunt 'urt once in a while, does it?

Dave   Yeah. Dunt 'urt no one.

Pause.

Sorry 'bout that.

Gonzo   Don't be fuckin' . . .

Dave   No, yer know? Just get stupid innit?

Pause.

Gonzo   Want another? 'Ere.

Gonzo *digs in his pocket, pulls out a rock.*

Dave   On tik like? Fuckin' skint.

Gonzo   Whenever, star, whenever.

Gonzo *lights and smokes the pipe.*

Dave   Be fuckin' good wunt it? Go on 'oliday again like. Sail out t'Dam. Me n'you. Be great wunt it, Gonz?

Gonzo *passes the pipe to* **Dave**.
Dave *smokes.*
Long pause.

Dave (*to* **Lucy**)   You alright? See owt yer like?

Lucy   Quilt covers.

Dave   Yeah?

Lucy   Look.

Dave *looks at the catalogue.*

Dave   Got everythin' at Argos, 'ant they?

Lucy   Yeah.

Dave   Just gotta tap in the numbers.

Lucy   Yeah.

Dave *winks at* **Gonzo**.

Dave   Go there later then can't we?

Lucy *holds* **Dave***'s hand, flicking through the catalogue.*
Pause.

Dave   'Ere, Gonz. Gonzo.

Gonzo   What?

Dave   Looks good, dunt she?

Gonzo   S'ppose.

Dave *feels* **Lucy***'s belly.*

Dave   Can feel it movin' sometimes. 'Ere.

He takes the catalogue off **Lucy**.

Go on. Touch it.

Gonzo   Eh?

Lucy   Dave!

Dave   Go on.

Gonzo   What? Yer sure, like?

Lucy   'Ant finished yet.

Dave   Gonzo.

Pause.
Gonzo *puts his hand on* **Lucy***'s belly.*

Gonzo   Alright that, int it?

Dave   Can yer feel owt?

Gonzo   Not really.

Dave   Notice the way 'er lips've come up. All full like.

Gonzo   Oh yeah.

Dave   And 'er skin's cleared up.

Gonzo   Fuck.

Dave   Run yer fingers through 'er 'air. Like this. Won't bite or nothin'.

Gonzo *does as he is told.*

Dave   'Ant washed it all week either. What d'yer think?

Gonzo   Nice. Very clean.

Dave   Nature's way that. Just the fuckin' mind that's problem. All those chemicals rushin' through 'er brain like Nigel bloody Mansell.

Gonzo   D'yer mind if I . . . ?

Dave   No, go f'yer life like.

Gonzo *feels* **Lucy***'s belly.*

Dave   Gonna tek after 'is dad, I swear. Size of it already.

Gonzo   Might be twins.

Dave   One for each tit, yer mean.

Gonzo *pulls his hand away.*

Gonzo   Yeah, it's good that.

Dave   Fuckin' look at 'em. Look at 'em.

He grabs **Lucy***'s tits.*

Oooh. 'Ave some o'that, mate. None o'yer semi-skimmed shite in these bastards.

Gonzo (*laughs*)   You're fucked.

Dave   Naow. Just natural int it, love?

Lucy *spits in* **Dave***'s face.*
Pause.

Dave   Shunt o'done that.

Lucy   Why?

Dave   Yer know why.

Lucy   Why?

Dave   If yer've got any sense, yer'd . . .

Lucy   Why?

Pause.

Dave   Dirty fuckin' . . .

Lucy   I 'ate you sometimes.

Dave   . . . slut.

Lucy   Treat place like an 'otel.

Dave   I fuckin' wish.

Lucy   Both of yers. Sick o'doin' your dirty work every day.
State o'the place.

She wrenches herself to her feet.

Well?

Gonzo *and* **Dave** *smoke.*
Pause.

Lucy   When yer fuckin' ready then, eh?

Lucy *goes to the paint pots. She takes the rollerbrush and starts
painting, very awkwardly.*

Pause.

Dave   'Ere, shall we get off?

Gonzo   Eh?

Dave Can't we go t'yours or somert?

Gonzo Yer jokin', aren't yer? Jocy'd do 'er nut.

Dave Well, I can't stay 'ere – 'Ey! What 'ave I told yer 'bout that? F'fucksake, Lucy!

Lucy *is painting the wall, very haphazardly.*

Dave Unfuckin'believable this.

He gets up and moves to **Lucy**.

What 'ave I told yer?

Lucy We're s'pposed t'be a family.

Dave We are.

Lucy Dunt feel like it. Dunt feel like owt no more. Sat on yer big fat arse. Get a job 'e sez.

Dave I'm tryin'.

Lucy In yer dreams.

Dave There int nothin' goin', Luce.

Lucy 'Ant even looked.

Dave Yer don't know what it's like out there. Grown man like me, can't even get a job stacking shelves. It's humiliatin', Luce. Talked down to by kids 'alf my age.

Lucy I'm 'alf your age.

Dave What?

Lucy That 'ow yer feel about me, is it? Humiliated? Shamed to even tek me out the 'ouse case someone sees.

Dave No.

Lucy 'Cause that's 'ow it fuckin' feels.

Dave Oh, come on, Luce, yer just bein' stupid now.

Lucy Yeah, well, 'ow's it gonna be when we 'ave guests round eh? What they gonna think with shit all over the floor?

No fuckin' money, no nothin'. Pinocchio there, sat like a ferret. It's not normal, Dave.

Dave   Lucy.

Lucy   I 'ate it. Fuckin' chose this colour and it just sits there growin' skin.

Dave   Yer not even rollin' it right. It's up n'down, Luce, not sideways. Up n'down. F'fucksake, give it 'ere . . .

He grabs **Lucy***'s painting arm. She refuses to stop.*

Be'ave, will yer?! Lucy!

Lucy *turns, smearing* **Dave***'s face with the rollerbrush.*

Dave   Jesus . . .

Lucy *giggles, there is a slight struggle,* **Dave** *knocks the roller out of her hand.*

Dave   Fuckin' . . .

Lucy*, giggling, backs away, holding the tin of paint.* **Dave** *wipes the paint out of his eyes.*

Dave   Little . . . !

He approaches **Lucy***, who starts flicking paint at him.*

'Ey!

Lucy*, giggling, backs across the room, flicking paint at* **Dave***, who moves after her.* **Gonzo** *jumpily avoids the paint, protecting the crackpipe.*

Dave   One more, fuckin' . . . I'm warnin' yer, Luce . . . Gimme the . . .

Dave *grabs* **Lucy** *by the hair.*

Lucy   Ow!!

Dave *pulls the can of paint out of* **Lucy***'s hand.*

Dave   D'yer know 'ow much that cost me?!

Dave *lets go of* **Lucy**, *marches across the room and puts the tin of paint back by the wall.*

Lucy   You're no fun, you.

Dave   Should fuckin' certify yer! Brand new shirt.

He exits into the bathroom, slamming the door.
Pause.

Dave (*off*)   Christ!

Gonzo *prepares his crackpipe.*
Pause.

Gonzo   Want some o'this? (*Pause.*) There's enough, like.

Lucy   Eh?

Gonzo   'Ello. Earth callin' Lucy.

Lucy   What?

Gonzo   Want some o'this? 'Ave t'be quick about it mind. 'Ere.

Lucy *sits.*
Gonzo *passes the pipe and the lighter to* **Lucy**.

Gonzo   Just tek it slow, yeah? Let it linger in yer mouth. Like a cigar or somert. (*Pause.*) Well, go on then.

Lucy *lights the rock and takes her first pull.*

Gonzo   Slowly. That's it.

Pause.
Lucy *takes another pull.*

Gonzo   Alright, alright, int bloody Olympics.

Gonzo *takes the pipe. He quickly adds cigarette ash to the bowl.*
Pause.
Lucy *sits back. Ever so slowly she exhales the smoke.*
Long pause.

Gonzo   Nowt tastes like this shit. Lingers in yer gob like
. . . Like palm o'violets or somert. (*Pause.*) Good, yeah? Never
forget that either.

He digs in his pocket and pulls out a scrap of paper.

Keep it under yer 'at though, yeah?

Lucy *takes the paper. She strokes* **Gonzo***'s nose. He grabs her hand.*

Gonzo   'Ey. What 'ave I said about that.

Lucy   Worried what 'e'll say?

Pause.

Think you own this place, don't yer?

The bathroom door opens. **Gonzo** *grabs the scrap of paper out of*
Lucy*'s hand and stuffs it in his pocket.*

Dave *enters. He moves to the bed and sits.*

Dave   'Ey. (*Pause.*) Lucy. Lucy.

Lucy   What?

Dave   Come 'ere.

Pause.

It'll get done, alright? Promise.

Lucy   Said that last time.

Dave   I mean it. I'll gi'Bill a ring. Must be somert goin'.
Sweep up the fuckin' sawdust if I 'ave to. Promise.

Pause.
Lucy *wrenches herself up and moves to* **Dave***. She sits on the bed.*
Gonzo *carries on regardless. Pause.*

Lucy   Strip off then.

Dave   Eh?

Lucy   'Cause. Just cuddle n'that.

Dave   But . . .

Lucy   Won't say owt will yer, Gonz? (*Pause.*) See? Go on.

Dave *laughs.* **Lucy** *laughs with him.*

Lucy   Go on.

Dave   Not on me own I'm not.

Lucy   Wanna see.

Dave   Gi'oer.

Lucy   Wanna see now. Please.

Pause.

Dave   Gi'us a blow job, like.

Lucy   No.

Dave   I'll gi'you one.

Lucy   No, Dave.

Dave   Dunt make sense otherwise.

Lucy   Give 'im one if yer don't.

Dave   What?

Lucy   I will won't I, Gonz? Probably bigger than yours anyway.

Long pause. **Dave** *and* **Lucy** *laugh / giggle.*

Dave   Come 'ere you.

Dave *holds* **Lucy**.

Lucy   Can 'ear 'im, Dave.

Dave   Mm?

Lucy   Listen. Can 'ear 'im.

Long pause.

Dave   Sometimes feel like cryin'. Yer know?

Lights fade.

Scene Five

Five months later. Night.

The flat is decorated with balloons, streamers, and a banner pinned up on the backwall, which reads 'CONGRATULATIONS!'

Lucy *and* **Jo** *sit on the floor, playing Cluedo.* **Lucy** *wears a nightie and has a hospital band strapped to her wrist. Her feet and ankles are stained with mud and dirt.* **Lucy** *pulls the cards out of the little black envelope.*

Lucy   Ah, see that's where yer wrong. It were the spanner not the rope.

Jo   Oh well. Never mind, eh?

Lucy   Must be a card missin'.

Jo   Yes.

Lucy   Shall we 'ave another?

Jo   I don't think we've got time, dear.

Lucy   Course we 'ave! All the time in the world, come on.

Jo *takes her mobile phone out of her handbag.*

Lucy   Come on, Gran.

Jo *dials a number, waits for an answer.*
Lucy *sets up the pieces for another game of Cluedo.*

Lucy   Just upset yer lost, aren't yer? It's only a game.

Jo   'Ello, Nikki? . . . Where? . . . Well, 'urry up about it will yer? . . . Yes. . . . Yes, I know it's . . . Tell 'im to put 'is foot down then.

Jo *turns the phone off.*

Lucy   Cheer up.

Jo   Why d'yer do it, eh? Lucy?

Lucy   You playin' or what?

Jo   Like that.

Lucy   What?

Jo   Dressed like that. In the middle o'the bloody night?

Lucy   Took a short cut through woods.

Jo   Been worried sick.

Lucy   I was bored.

Jo   It's got to stop, Lucy.

Lucy   It's got to stop, Lucy.

Jo   There's a baby back there needs its mother.

Lucy   Gi'it one then.

Jo   What?

Lucy   A mother, gi'it a mother.

Jo   Should wring your bloody neck.

Lucy   Like an ostrich. Neck like an ostrich.

Jo   I give up.

Lucy   That's what the teachers used t'say.

Jo   Yeah, there were some said a lot o'bloody things.

Lucy   Taught me more than you ever did. Don't stare. Don't stare, I said. Worse than them Harold bloody Shipmans, treat me like a geriatric. Can fuckin' stuff their needles. Stuff 'em up their arse. Try n'take me away, well? Sit down if yer stayin'.

Jo   Yer sister'll be 'ere in a minute.

Lucy   I'm not movin'.

Jo   You haven't got a choice, Luce. You can't just . . .

Lucy   Fuckin' make it then!

Jo   Eh?

Lucy   A game, let's play another game, Gran.

Jo   If 'e comes, if 'e finds yer 'ere . . .

Lucy   Borin'.

Jo   Took five of 'em to hold 'im down back there. You heard him, Lucy.

Lucy   'E'll come round.

Jo   Not now 'e won't.

Lucy   Always do. Yer don't know 'im, Gran, what 'e's like. I writ 'im a letter n'everythin'. On the side there.

Jo *finds the letter. She scans through it.*

Lucy   Weren't my fault. Weren't anyone's fault really. I mean, every couple 'as its ups n'downs.

Jo   Pack o'bloody lies.

Lucy   Be back on our feet in no time.

Jo   Should be ashamed of yerself.

Lucy   In no time. Yer'll see. More to life than this. What yer feel that counts. What's between us. What none o'you ever fuckin' see.

Pause.

If Darren was 'ere he'd play. Break 'is arm for me 'e would.

Jo   Oh darlin'.

She embraces **Lucy***, kisses her.*

What happened, eh?

Lucy   Giv'oer, Gran! I'm not a kid.

Pause.

What?

Jo   Come on. Let's get you dressed, eh?

She moves to the chest of drawers and removes items of clothing.

Surprised yer never freezed to death.

Lucy   Wish you'd make up yer mind. Thought we were gonna play.

Jo   Once we get 'ome.

Lucy   I am 'ome.

Pause.

Jo   She is a beautiful little thing.

Lucy *shrugs.*

Jo   Just need t'spend some time together, that's all.

Lucy   'Er 'ead throbs.

Jo   What?

Lucy   Dint wanna girl anyway.

Jo   Oh, come on . . .

Lucy   Not what we need though, is it? Another fuckin' cunt in the family.

Jo   'Ey!

Lucy   Well . . .

Jo   Don't you ever speak about our . . .

Lucy   It's true.

Jo   . . . family like that again, you 'ear?! (*Pause.*) After all we've been through, Lucy, f'Chrissakes.

Pause.
Jo *takes* **Lucy***'s socks, tries fitting them on* **Lucy***'s feet.* **Lucy** *struggles, laughing.*

Lucy (*giggling*)   What yer doin'? Gran!

Jo   I've already told you, dear, yer sister's going to be . . .

Lucy   Gran! Stop it, will yer?!

Jo   You bloody do it then.

Lucy   Yer ticklin' me!

Jo *moves away, as* **Lucy** *laughs.* **Jo** *tries ringing* **Nikki** *again.*
Pause.

Lucy   Don't stop.

Pause.

Wish we'd played like this before. Gran? Gran.

Jo (*to the phone*)   Come on, come on . . .

Lucy *starts sorting the Cluedo cards into piles.*

Lucy   Be mad if they were real, wunt it? Real people, I mean. Looks like you that Mrs White.

Jo *turns the phone off.*
Pause.
Jo *sits on the bed, watching* **Lucy**, *who sorts through the cards.*
Pause.

Jo   Can see why they fall at yer feet.

Lucy (*absently*)   Eh?

Jo   Take after yer mother.

Pause.

Hm. I weren't no cream tea either.

Lucy   It's Nikki I worry about.

Jo   I know how yer feel, Lucy. Really I do.

Lucy   What d'yer want, a medal?

Longer pause.

Jo   Could o'done more couldn't I? Yer can say it. I know. (*Pause.*) We all miss 'er, Lucy. (*Pause.*) Goin' to make it up t'yer n'all. Yer'll see. (*Pause.*) Just . . . Just tell me what . . .

Lucy   There. I've done it, look. It's the ballroom that's gone. (*Pause.*) You alright? (*Pause.*) Stupid game anyway. Everyone's got computers now, 'ant they?

Jo   Is that what yer'd like?

Lucy   Eh?

Jo   Brendan's got a computer.

Lucy   Who?

Jo   Nikki's boyfriend. Ask 'im nicely 'e might lend you it.

Lucy   Is 'e handsome?

Jo   Depends.

Lucy   Depends what yer mean by handsome?

Jo   Not really.

Lucy   Oh. She does love 'im though, dunt she?

Jo   There'll be 'ere soon anyway. Yer should ask her.

Lucy   She'll just laugh. I like the way she laughs.

Pause.

Dave's handsome int 'e? It's the skin. Constant. Like varnish. Wunt be seen dead wi'no ugly bloke. Not outside anyway. Not wi'everyone pointin'. All pink n'blemished n'all the wrong clothes.

Jo   Sound like yer grandad.

Lucy   Shall we play hide n'seek? Be good that. Before 'e gets back. You hide, and I'll count to sixty.

Jo   He's not coming back, Lucy.

Lucy   What?

Jo   He's not coming anywhere.

Lucy   'Course he is. Always does.

Jo   Not any more.

Lucy   Gettin' married in the spring. We are. We are. I thought yer knew.

Jo   Help yer buy a dress if yer want.

Lucy   Would yer?

Jo   Go town together. That shop by Debenhams.

Lucy   Big white thing in the window?

Jo   Yes.

Lucy   With a veil?

Jo   With a veil.

Lucy   Oh.

Jo   Can't go dressed like that.

Lucy   Yer can be a bridesmaid if yer want.

Jo   Well . . .

Lucy   Make my day that.

Jo   I'm a bit old to be a bridesmaid, dear.

Lucy   No yer not. No such thing as age. Long as yer wear contact lenses.

Jo   It's your day.

Lucy   You got married, dint yer?

Jo   Wasn't much choice with my parents.

Lucy   I know what yer mean. (*Pause.*) Remember 'e used to 'ave tongue in 'is sandwiches. (*Pause.*) Did yer ever go on honeymoon?

Jo   Blackpool.

Lucy   Pleasure beach n'that. We're gonna go Jamaica.

Jo   Lovely.

Lucy   On the beach. Where Bob grew up.

Jo   Get a nice tan.

Lucy   Yeah. That or Spain. Dunt make sense stayin' 'ere.
All the same in this country. Never feel like yer've gone
nowhere. Too many people. Too small.

Jo   You're cold, aren't you? I am.

Lucy   No gas.

Jo   Freezin'.

Lucy   Really? Should light some candles.

Jo   Put some clothes on more like.

Lucy   Yer gonna stay? You never stay, not once.

Jo   I am now.

Lucy   Would yer?

Jo   'Ere.

She takes the clothes off the bed and moves to **Lucy**.

Make yer look beautiful. Come on.

She lifts **Lucy** *up.*

Lucy   Need some make-up.

Jo   One thing at a time.

She dresses **Lucy**.
Pause.

Look at yer. Should never 'ave let yer go in first place.

Lucy   Could bottle me up n'sell us as perfume, cunt yer? Or
pop. Fizzy pop.

Jo   I'm not gonna watch same 'appen t'you, Lucy, I'm not.
You 'ear me? Not again.

Lucy   Wunt be enough to go round though, would there
really?

Jo   Likes o'that idiot, treatin' yer like a . . . Like that, like meat and for what?

Lucy   'E will come back, won't 'e, Gran?

Jo   Could be so bloody simple.

Lucy   Won't be the same otherwise.

Jo   I dunno. Someone should bomb this bloody country. That'd wake us up a bit. Saddam Hussein or someone. IRA, bleedin' whatsisface? Bin Laden. Yeah. He could do it. Drop a few tons of anthrax. Teach us what it really means to suffer.

Lucy   D'yer wanna pick me? Pick me spots. Got tons o'black'eads, me. Deep down. Be like monkeys, won't we?

Jo *strokes* **Lucy**'*s face.*

Jo   Hm. Sweet.

Pause.

Lucy   I like that.

Pause.

Dave *enters through the front door, with a bag.*

Lucy   See? Told yer dint I?

Jo   You stay away from 'er, 'ear?

Dave *ignores* **Jo** *and starts moving round the room, collecting his belongings (mainly clothes) and stuffing them in the bag.*

Lucy   Dave?

Jo   Come on.

Lucy   Dave, what's wrong?

Jo   Put yer jacket on.

Lucy   I writ yer a letter, Dave, look.

Jo   Come on. Put it on, Lucy.

Jo *tries draping the jacket on* **Lucy**, **Lucy** *pushes her away.*

Lucy   Geddof me! Dave . . .

She tries approaching **Dave**, *who carries on regardless.*

Dave, please, talk to me. Talk to me, Dave.

Pause.

Just bein' silly now.

Jo   Leave it.

Pause.

Lucy   D'yer want some ice cream? Dave? It's yer favourite.

Lucy *exits into the kitchen.*
Pause.
Dave *finishes packing his bag.*

Jo   Yer thought what yer gonna do?

Dave *finishes packing his bag.*
Lucy *re-enters with a bowl of ice cream and a spoon.*

Lucy   'Ere we are. Great big oofus.

Dave *takes the bowl of ice cream. Doesn't move.*
Pause.

Dave   Does 'e know?

Lucy   What?

Dave   Does 'e know?

Lucy   What yer talkin' 'bout? Sit down. Sit down, Dave.
'Ant seen yer in days. Look at the balloons look.

Jo *takes the bowl of ice cream off* **Dave**, *escorts him to the door.*

Lucy   Gran! 'E 'ant even started yet. Tell 'er, Dave. 'E 'ant
even started. 'E 'ant even started.

Dave *exits.*

Lucy   Dave! Dave, wait!

She grabs her letter, exits, running after **Dave**.

Lucy (*off*) Dave!

Pause.
Jo *sits on the bed. The mobile phone rings. She sighs, and takes her glasses off. The mobile phone stops ringing.*
Lucy *re-enters, slamming the door, holding the letter.*

Jo   Can 'ardly blame 'im for being upset, Lucy.

Lucy   You told 'im, dint yer?

Jo   Told 'im?

Lucy   Were you.

Jo   Told 'im what?

Lucy   All along.

Jo   It were bloody obvious, Luce.

Lucy   Should o'known.

Jo   Only 'ad to look at 'er!

Lucy   Old fuckin' four-eyed cunt!

Jo   Only had to look at 'er, Lucy. What's wrong with yer? You expect him to just change overnight? It's not my fault, Lucy, you knew.

Lucy   Liar.

Jo   You knew what was going to –

Lucy   Yer always lyin'.

Jo   Look, say what yer like, Lucy, you just say what –

Lucy   I will.

Jo   Yer livin' in a dream world!

Lucy   Done it now. Done it now, 'ant yer?

Jo   F'Chrissakes –

Lucy   Useless fuckin' –

Jo   Don't blame me f'your fuckin' –

Lucy   That why yer told 'im? Jealous bitch.

Jo   I never said anything!

Lucy   Bet yer 'ant been fucked in yonks, 'ave yer?

Jo   What? . . . F'Chrissakes, he's not an idiot, Lucy, he's –

Lucy   Buttin' in. Ruin' everythin'. Mum, Nikki, me – Think yer fuckin' Gandhi or somert.

Jo   That's enough.

Lucy   Think yer fuckin' Gandhi, keep us for yersen. Yeah, must be 'ard at your age. Waitin' to die like that. Buried alive.

Jo   Yeah . . .

Lucy   Buried alive! Crap! Rotten fuckin' crap!

Jo   Yeah, well wait till they catch sight o'you, dear. Dirt like you with . . . with death written all over yer.

Lucy   Yeah?

Jo   Whore. Waste o'fuckin' space –

Lucy   Arrrr.

Jo   You and yer docile bloody sister! All I've done, all the time I've wasted.

Lucy   Come on then –

Jo   Not worth the ground she walked upon, neither of yer, pair o' bloody –

Lucy *yanks* **Jo**'s *glasses and throws them.*

Lucy   Makes us even then dunt it, love?

Jo *tries to move,* **Lucy** *stops her.*

Lucy   'Bout all yer good for.

Lucy *grabs* **Jo** *by the head and kisses her.* **Jo** *struggles.* **Lucy** *bites* **Jo**'s *lip.* **Jo** *screams.*

Lucy   Should put yer in a zoo lookin' like that. Pig.

Jo   Lucy, please, I can't see a –

Lucy   Pig!

She slaps **Jo**.

Mek me sick just lookin' at yer, pig.

She slaps **Jo** *repeatedly across the face. The slaps turn into blows with her fist.*

Lucy (*as she strikes*)   Pig, pig, pig, pig, pig, pig. Last f'you, pig! Last f'you!

Lucy *grabs* **Jo** *and pushes her to the ground.*

Blackout.

Scene Six

Three weeks later. Day.

Lucy *in bed.*
Darren *sits on the edge, getting dressed.*

Lucy   Did 'urt a bit.

Darren   Should o'said somert then, shunt yer?

Pause.

Lucy   Thought yer liked it.

Darren   Worried it'll bruise?

Lucy   Thought yer liked it.

Darren   I did. Shuddup about it, will yer?

Pause.

Lucy   Yer will come back, won't yer?

Darren   'Course.

Lucy   Not just sayin' that.

Darren   No.

Lucy   People say things, see?

Darren   Not me.

Lucy   That's what I like about you.

Pause.

Gettin' disability allowance now. What wi'me back n'that.

Darren   Oh. That's 'andy.

Lucy   Tell 'em anythin', me. Talk me way out of owt.
Never change, do I?

Pause.

Darren   Whose was it then?

Pause.
Lucy *kisses* **Darren**.

Darren   Whose was it?

Lucy *kisses* **Darren**.
Pause.

Darren   Look. I know it's not really your thing, but . . .

*He reaches into his jeans pocket and pulls out a Pentecostal Church
pamphlet, gives it to* **Lucy**.

When yer've got time. When yer've got a day free. Give us a
ring. We're all friends. Think yer'll be surprised.

Pause.

Lucy   Yer will come back though, won't yer, Darren? Yer
will come back? Say yer'll come back. Come back.

Lights fade.

Scene Seven

Night. Late December.

The flat is practically bare. The curtains are open. Two large heavy bin bags on the bed. **Lucy** *fills up the bin bags with her junk.* **Nikki** *stands in the open doorway.*

Lucy   Thought yer'd bin abducted. Sucked up on a flyin' saucer or somert.

Nikki   What d'yer want, Luce?

Lucy   Oh, cheer up, yer ninny, I'm only jokin'. D'yer want a cup o'tea?

Nikki   No ta.

Lucy   Are you alright? Yer don't look alright.

Nikki   Bin up since five this mornin'.

Lucy   Arrr. Mek a brew if yer want. Stood there like a bloody tent peg, sit down.

Nikki   I've gotta get back.

Lucy   Five minutes int gonna hurt yer. Go on.

Nikki   'Ad to tek 'er round the neighbours, Luce. They're not 'appy about it neither. Bad enough 'er cryin' mornin', noon n'night keepin' the whole street up without me dumpin' 'er on total strangers n'all. It's not fair, Luce. She won't stop.

Lucy   Med up me mind, Nik.

Nikki   Don't give a fuck, d'yer?

Lucy   Alright, alright, don't get yer knickers in a twist. 'Ant even told yer yet.

Nikki   What?

Lucy   Was thinkin' about robbin' the Chinky. (*Pause.*) I'm jokin'. God, can't yer take a joke no more?

Nikki   Not when it comes out o'your mouth, no.

Lucy   Well, yer'll 'ave to get used to it, sis. I'm comin' 'ome.

Nikki   What?

Lucy   Mad innit. Gran was right. Best thing really. Thought yer'd be surprised. Just decided, like. Be great, won't it? Just like the old days.

Nikki   And that's why yer dragged me over 'ere, is it?

Lucy   Yeah. 'Elp us carry me stuff, can't yer?

Nikki   You are jokin' aren't yer?

Lucy   Free country. Do what I like. Get the bus can't we?

Nikki   You're not right. You need a doctor.

Lucy   Doctor Who. 'Ere, d'yer like me trainers? Cost a bomb, like. Whole bloody giro. Typical. Typical me. Go n'treat mesen n'I leave meself skint. Good though, aren't they? Adidas. Go wi'me socks, don't they? Green. Like little Christmas trees.

Nikki   Don't bloody need this.

Lucy   Long as I keep 'em clean.

Nikki   You must think I'm mad.

Lucy   What?

Gonzo *enters, holding a crappy microwave in his arms. He kicks the front door open.*

Gonzo   Fucksake! Killer those stairs, innit?

He dumps the microwave down.

'Ere, don't move, alright? Jocy's doin' 'er nut.

Gonzo *exits.*
Lucy *inspects the microwave.*

Lucy   Ooh. That's nice, int it? Go well in the kitchen that. Yer still got that calendar with all the kittens on it? Am serious, Nik.

Nikki   Yeah.

Lucy   Start again like. The two of us.

Nikki   In yer fuckin' dreams we will.

Lucy   Oh, come on, don't be like that.

Nikki   After what you did to Gran? After you put 'er in a fuckin' . . . ?!

Lucy   Since when? No. No, yer wrong, I . . .

Nikki   Should lock you up.

Lucy   Never touched 'er!

Nikki   Little bitch.

Lucy   I never touched 'er! Please, Nikki. Come on, let's not fight, not now. Sure yer don't want a cup o'tea?

Nikki   She's not comin' back, Luce.

Lucy   Eh?

Nikki   They're gonna put 'er in an 'ome.

Lucy   No they're not.

Nikki   She can 'ardly even talk straight! Whole right side of 'er . . . 'Cause o'you.

Lucy   Naow.

Nikki   Cunt 'ardly recognise 'er at first. Drinkin' out this little plastic cup they give 'er. Funnel on side, like. Wipin' 'er mouth every two seconds. And them, wheelin' 'er down ward like an astronaut forra bath. Can't even go the bog wi'out some – Are you smilin'?

Lucy   Don't be stupid.

Nikki   Think it's fuckin' funny?

Lucy   No!

Nikki   All she ever does is ask about you n'all. N'there's me stood like . . . like I'm invisible or somert, 'avin' to lie on your be'alf.

Lucy   Never asked yer to.

Nikki   Lucky she never pressed no charges.

Lucy   I won't bother you or owt.

Nikki   What?

Lucy   Just stay in me room if yer want.

Nikki   Jesus Christ, are you fuckin' deaf?

Lucy   I'll 'elp with the washin'-up n'that.

Nikki   What, while I look after the baby?

Lucy   No.

Nikki   S'ppose we'll draw up a rota then, yeah?

Lucy   Whatever.

Nikki   Long as you're 'appy.

Lucy   Yeah. All of us. Simple, int it?

Nikki   Yeah.

Lucy   Yeah. Get a job or somert.

Nikki   What? Finally goin' on game, are yer? 'Bout all yer bloody good for.

Pause.

Well. It's true, innit?

Lucy   No, I mean it, Nikki. I'll go college or somert. Promise.

Nikki   Look . . .

Lucy   Cross me 'eart, Nik.

Nikki   It's too late anyway, Luce.

Pause.

Movin' in wi'Brendan, aren't I? 'Im n'is dad. Said they'd put us up forra bit while I . . .

Lucy   Since when?

Nikki   F'fucksake, Luce . . .

Lucy   Yer can't do that!

Nikki   I'm doin' it.

Lucy   Yer can't.

Nikki   Got no other choice, 'ave I?

Lucy   Yes you 'ave.

Nikki   I can barely afford the rent, Luce.

Lucy   We'll pay it together, won't we?

Nikki   Don't be stupid.

Lucy   I'll get a job.

Nikki   Yer livin' in a dream world!

Pause.

There's room there, there's space, Luce. Goin' mad back there, on me own, bloody social knockin' on the door every five seconds, it's . . . It's too much. I can't handle it no more, look at me! I fuckin' hate you. What you've done to me, it's not fair! You n'yer fuckin' baby. Feel like flushin' it down the bog sometimes.

Pause.

Surprised you even know 'er name.

Pause.

Lucy   She alright?

Nikki   Since when 'ave you bin bothered? Yeah. Yeah, she's . . . Over 'er cold anyway.

Lucy   Oh. Well, that's good.

Nikki   Gonna tek 'er to Whirlow Farm next week. Tek t'see the cows n'that. Brendan's gonna drive us there at the weekend. Come along if yer want.

Lucy   Went there wi'school once.

Pause.

Be good though, wunt it?

Nikki   Eh?

Lucy   Me n'you. Be good. Be like that song. (*Pause, signals to the bags.*) Fuckin' psycho, me, aren't I? Eh? Fuckin' psycho bird.

Pause.

D'yer love 'im?

Nikki   Yeah? (*Pause.*) Yeah. When 'e's not talkin' shit. (*Pause.*) Once in a blue moon.

Pause.

Lucy   Might just go the pictures anyway. There's a cinema in Barnsley, 'ave a fag n'everythin'.

Nikki   'Ant bin the pictures in ages.

Lucy   No. Me neither. Bit o'freedom, innit?

Nikki   Yeah.

Pause.

Should 'ave a bath.

Lucy   'Ow come like?

Nikki   'Cause yer stink?

Lucy   No I don't.

Nikki   Yer bloody do n'all.

Nikki *gets up, exits into the bathroom.*

Lucy *sits motionless.*
The bath taps are turned on, offstage.

Lucy   Yerra good girl, Nikki!

Nikki (*off*)   Eh?

Pause.

Nikki *re-enters, shutting the door behind her.*

Nikki   What yer say?

Gonzo *enters, quickly, out of breath.*

Gonzo   Honestly, Luce, these people are fuckin' scumbags. (*Pause.*) Oh, alright. This a mate o'yours, is it?

Nikki   We're sisters.

Gonzo   Not interruptin' owt, am I?

Pause.

Tek that as a no then, yeah? 'Ere . . . (*Taps the roof of the microwave.*) . . . what d'yer think? Same bloke gi'us the telly.

Lucy   Yeah.

Gonzo   Dial's a bit wonky like.

Nikki (*to* **Lucy**)   Listen, are you gonna be OK?

Gonzo   Name's Gonzo, by the way.

He extends his hand. **Nikki** *freezes.*
Pause.

Gonzo   I'm not a bloody leper or nothin'.

Nikki   That's 'im, innit?

Gonzo   What? (*To* **Lucy**.) She a bit . . . ? (*Pause.*) Fuck me, yer ever see that film, *Night of the Livin' Dead*?

Gonzo *pulls a can of Coke out of his jacket and lights a fag.*

Nikki   'Ere. Don't forget yer bath, eh?

Lucy   Thanks.

Nikki   I'll pop round in a day or two.

Lucy   Yeah.

Gonzo   Good t'meet yer, yeah?

Nikki *exits.*

Gonzo   Yeah, and you. Bloody 'ell, barrel o'laughs that one, int she?

He takes rocks, pipe, etc., out of his jacket and starts building a crackpipe.

Can't stay long meself actually, fuckin' . . . People lettin' me down, yer know? Fuckin' schmeigals. Make me wanna . . . blow up, star. Just 'avin' t'smell 'em, it's like . . . Words can't describe it, yer know? Dogshit all oer landin'. Needles everywhere, fuckin' . . . Three 'en'em wi'this Greek bird. Fuck knows 'ow she got mixed up wi'them. S'pposed t'be studyin' or somert. Sat in corner wi'the shakes like. Breaks yer 'eart. And them all fuckin' mouth. Givin' off like fuckin' Oasis, tryin' t'scam us like I'm some sort o'dial-a-fuckin'-skag. Burnin' up me wallet, star. Me, a grown man. Wife n'kid t'support.

Pause.

Can keep that.

Pause.
He lights and smokes his pipe.
Long pause.

'Ere. Yer don't mind, do yer?

Lucy   What?

Gonzo *offers the pipe to* **Lucy**.

Gonzo   Look like yer could do with it.

Lucy *hesitates.*

Gonzo   Well, go on. Pack up yer troubles.

Gonzo *passes* **Lucy** *the pipe.* **Lucy** *smokes.*
Long pause.
Lucy *and* **Gonzo** *sit sharing the pipe.*

Gonzo   Lot more where that came from n'all.

Pause.

Like yer trainers.

Lucy   D'yer?

Gonzo   Yeah. Good colour n'that. They new?

Gonzo *starts loading another pipe.*

Lucy   Love me trainers me.

Gonzo   Mind if I bring a mate o'mine round next time.

Lucy   Who?

Gonzo   Mate o'mine. I were tellin' 'im about you today.
Wants to meet yer like. Good bloke actually. (*Pause.*) That
alright?

Lucy   Yeah? 'Course.

Gonzo   You on the Pill?

Lucy   Eh?

Gonzo   No, just . . . Yer know?

Pause.

Lucy   Look after mesen, can't I?

Gonzo   That's alright then. Long as yer know.

Lucy   My life.

Gonzo   Where've yer bin anyway? Bin knockin' all day.

Lucy   Eh?

Gonzo   Yer goin' somewhere? What's wi'all the luggage?

Lucy   Nothin'. Just thought.

Gonzo   What?

Lucy   Went round Darren's earlier.

Gonzo   'Oo?

Lucy   Weren't in anyway. Just lookin' through window. For ages like. Livin' room. Books. Plants. Carpet. Big leather sofa n'that. Pictures on walls. (*Pause.*) Must o'been out to a restaurant or somert. Fuckin' theatre. Sort o'thing they'd do innit? (*Pause.*) Just stood there. Ages like. Kept tellin' meself to move, but . . . (*Pause.*) They've got this fireplace, right? Coal. Fake fuckin' coal. (*Pause.*) Felt like pissin' on it.

Gonzo   'Ere.

He passes the pipe to **Lucy**.

Joan of bloody Arc.

Lucy *takes the pipe and smokes.*

Long pause.

Gonzo   'Av t'get off soon. Jocy's bought this iguana like. Scary fuckin' thing. Got a tub full o'locusts in the car. (*Pause.*) That is what they eat, int it?

Lucy   Got to eat somert.

She passes the pipe to **Gonzo**, *who smokes.*
Pause.
She rests.
Pause.

Got to eat somert. (*Pause. Chuckles.*) Locusts. (*Pause. Sighs.*) Oh. Fuck it.

Gonzo *finishes the pipe, sits back.*
Pause.

Lucy   Don't s'ppose yer fancy a game o' . . . ? Oh, yeah. Lizard. Forgot.

Pause.
She stares at **Gonzo**.

Professor Plum.

Gonzo   What?

Lucy *tenderly touches* **Gonzo***'s nose.*
Gonzo *pretends to hit her,* **Lucy** *flinches.*
Long pause.
Lucy *gets up and walks to the window.*

Gonzo   Sounds nice that place.

Lucy *peers out of the window.*

Lucy   Oh. It's snowin', look.

Pause.
She moves to **Gonzo**.

Look. Look, Gonz.

No response. **Lucy** *sits back down.*

Gonzo   Right.

He slowly sits up, pulling on his jacket.

That's it. I'm done. Yer gonna be alright? (*Pause.*) Yeah,
well . . .

He stands – headrush. He nearly stumbles over.

Oooh, fuck me. Fuckin' 'eadrush.

Lucy (*laughs*)   Eh?

Gonzo (*laughs*)   Jesus. Look at 'em.

Gonzo *starts clapping the space in front of him, as though killing flies.*
Lucy *laughs.*

Lucy   Gonzo.

Gonzo   Little bastards. Yer ever get that? Like gold dust or
somert. Microscopic angels.

He claps some more, then stops.

That's 'ow I know there's a Great Spirit like.

Lucy   What?

Gonzo   Great Spirit. Separate realities n'that. Carlos Castaneda. I'll lend you a book about it, if yer want. Tells yer how t'control yer dreams n'that. Consciously like. Shape shift. Them angels then? Messages from the other side. T'remind yer.

Lucy   Of what?

Gonzo   What's what, star, what's what. Why we're 'ere, yer know? Whole bloody point of it all. We're plannin' on goin' Mexico, like. Me n'Joce. Gonna try out some o'that peyote. Fly through clouds, like . . . (*Poses.*) Da-da-da-daaaah!

Lucy   Gi'us a kiss.

Gonzo   Eh?

Lucy   Gi'us a kiss.

Gonzo   And then what? I know what you're like.

Lucy   Go on.

Gonzo   I'm done wi'that remember?

Pause.

'Ere.

He digs in his pocket and pulls out two rocks wrapped in cling film.

So's yer don't get too bored.

He gives the rocks to **Lucy**.

Yeah?

Gonzo *kisses* **Lucy**.
Pause.

Lucy   Men.

Gonzo   What?

Lucy   Never give up, d'yer?

Pause.
Lucy *stares into space.*
Gonzo *gathers his things together – mobile phone, keys, etc.*

Lucy   Go the pictures.

Pause.

Gonzo   I'll pop round tomorrow, alright? (*Pause.*) Get that thing plugged in. Bit of a sesh. Just three of us, like, yeah? I mean . . . Yer not got owt planned 'ave yer? Yer'll still be 'ere, won't yer? Money t'be made.

Pause.

Oh, f'fucksake, Luce, cheer up.

Gonzo *exits.*
Long pause.
Sigh.

Lucy *eyes the microwave. She presses the button which opens the door, it 'bings'. She shuts the door. She opens it again, 'bing'.*

Pause.

Lucy *exits into the bathroom. Turns the taps off.*

Lucy *re-enters, shutting the bathroom door.*

Lucy *sits. She takes the crackpipe, cleans the gauze. She stops.*

Lucy *moves to the tape-recorder. She takes the cassette out, turns it over and presses play: Bob Marley.*

Lucy *stands, moves, sits, listens.*

Pause.

Lucy *moves to the tape-recorder, stops the tape. She takes the tape out and puts it in its box.*

Pause.

Lucy *sits. Stares into space.*

Pause.

Lucy *picks up the crackpipe, checks the gauze. She stops.*

Pause.

Lucy *rubs her head in her hands, wipes away the tears, sniffles. She hesitates, stops, hesitates, stops.*

Lucy *gets up, moves to the window, opens the curtains.*

Snow is falling.

Lucy *sits on the bed, stares out of the window, transfixed.*

Pause.

Lucy *scratches her head.*

Lights fade.

Lucky Dog

Lucky Dog was first performed at the Royal Court Theatre Upstairs, on 14 May 2004. The cast was as follows:

Eddie Alan Williams
Sue   Linda Bassett
Brett Liam Mills

Directed by James Macdonald
Designed by Jean Kalman
Lighting by Jean Kalman
Sound by Ian Dickinson

Characters

Eddie Webber, *fifties*
Sue Webber, *fifties*
Brett, *ten years old*

Settings

Scenes One to Three: Eddie and Sue's house in Sheffield. Christmas night.

Scenes Four to Ten: a beach in Fuerteventura, the Canary Islands. One year later, day.

Scene One: 5 p.m. Table, chairs and a Christmas tree.

Scene Two: 8 p.m. Table, chairs and a Christmas tree.

Scene Three: midnight. Table, chairs, Christmas tree and sofa chair. Television optional.

Scenes One to Three: fairy lights. No doors.

Scenes Four to Ten: two sunbeds. Beach umbrella. Sun and sand.

Scene One

Christmas Day. 5.00 p.m.

Eddie *and* **Sue** *sitting at the table eating Christmas dinner.*

Silence.

Sue Where'd yer take 'er?

Eddie Nowhere. Around. Up woods n' back.

Sue Won't eat 'er giblets.

Eddie She will.

Sue Can hardly stand, poor thing.

Silence.

Didn't hear yer leave. Were up n' about by eight. Must've left very early.

Eddie Not really.

Sue Had me worried, not a word all day. Thought yer might be in some bother.

Eddie No.

Sue Thought yer might be gone for good.

Silence.

Eddie Took 'er round park.

Sue Oh.

Eddie Round park f' ten minutes.

Sue Guessed as much.

Eddie Down Crabtree Pond. Up through woods. Over heliport n' back.

Sue You work that dog too hard.

Eddie She's alright.

Sue   Paw marks all over the carpet.

Eddie   She's not bothered.

Sue   Only bathed 'er Sunday, state of 'er already.

Silence.

Save me some o' them parsnips, won't yer?

Silence.

Many up there?

Eddie   Few.

Sue   That's nice.

Eddie   Couple o' terriers.

Sue   Oh.

Eddie   Staff.

Sue   Not many then.

Eddie   Not many. No.

Silence.

Retriever.

Sue   What?

Eddie   Golden retriever. Cone round its neck. Stop it scratchin'.

Sue   Oh dear.

Eddie   Skin infection.

Sue   Oh dear.

Silence.

Hope yer washed yer hands.

Eddie   Saw a robin.

Sue   What?

Eddie   Robin redbreast. Perched on bench by playground. Had to put 'er on lead, stop 'er chasin' it away. Tiny little thing.

Sue   Thought yer might've popped round Pam's.

Eddie   Ay.

Sue   Lovely fit.

Silence.

Does wonders f' yer waistline.

Eddie   Does it?

Sue   Seen it meself, in the window. TK Max. One o' the bargains.

Eddie   Oh.

Sue   In the bargain bin. Didn't think it were quite you. Didn't think it were quite your style.

Eddie   Didn't know I 'ad a style.

Sue   Not of yer own choosin', no.

Silence.

Very thoughtful of 'er.

Eddie   Ay.

Sue   Wunt want t' catch a chill.

Eddie   I won't.

Sue   How's she copin'?

Eddie   Oh. Yer know. Copin'.

Sue   You t' keep 'er company.

Silence.

Must be 'ard. This time o' year. All on 'er own.

Eddie   Dint mention it.

Sue   At her age.

Silence.

Eddie *pulls a Christmas card out of his back-pocket. He takes it out of its envelope and places it in the middle of the table.*

Eddie *eats.*

Silence.

Sue *takes the Chrsitmas card and examines it.*

Silence.

Good of her.

Eddie   Passed on yer regards.

Sue *places the Christmas card back on the table.*

Silence.

Sue   Hang it wi' the others can't we? Plenty o' room on the line.

Eddie   That's what it's there for.

Sue   That's what I thought.

Eddie   That's what it's there for.

Silence.

Sue   Had to put the caulies in wi' the sprouts. Used up every dish in the house.

Eddie   Oh.

Sue   Left it any longer they'd've turned t' bloody mush. 'Ad this thing on fifty degrees since three. Worried it might be too crisp.

Eddie   Nice n' tender.

Sue   D'yer want my skin?

Eddie   Ay.

Sue   Pass us yer plate.

Silence.

More gravy in the boat if yer want it.

Silence.

Yer missed the Queen's speech.

Eddie   Oh.

Sue   Yer didn't miss much. Yer know what she's like.

Silence.

Shed a few pounds since the op.

Eddie   Be dead come summer.

Sue   Expect she's got 'er hands full today. William n' Harry, bless. Squabbles round the table.

Eddie   Ay.

Sue   All the same at that age aren't they? Who gets to wear Granny's crown. Disappearing to their rooms every five minutes. The noise.

Silence.

Footsteps on the landin'.

Silence.

Surprised she's got the time f' the BBC.

Eddie   It's 'im.

Sue   What?

Eddie   Blair.

Sue   What about 'im?

Eddie   Do owt 'e bloody well says, she will.

Sue   Won't 'ear a word said against that man.

Eddie   . . .

Sue   Not today.

Eddie   (*mumbles*)   Bloody poodle.

Sue   What?

Silence.

Mumble.

Silence.

Weather says it's goin' t' snow tomorrow. If the weather's good.

Silence.

Thought we might drive over Chatsworth. Stop by that pub does the ploughman's.

Silence.

Sue   She'd like that.

Eddie   She would.

Sue   Put me wellies on, could walk 'er down the caves. Ladybower. Do us good, a change of scenery.

Silence.

Wear yer new whatsit.

Eddie   What?

Sue   What-yer-call-it.

Eddie   Fleece.

Sue   Wear it in.

Eddie   Ay.

Sue   Nothin' planned?

Silence.

I said yer've nothin' planned.

Eddie   No.

Sue   Well. That's settled then.

Silence.

Sue   Sure yer not too hot in that thing?

Silence.

Oh . . . Almost forgot.

Sue *offers* **Eddie** *her Christmas cracker.*

Sue   M an' S. They're ever so posh. Marks an' Sparks, look, come on.

Eddie *pulls* **Sue**'s *cracker.*

Sue   Leave it t' you we'd be recylin' last year's.

Sue *puts on her Christmas hat.*

Sue   Well? What d'yer think?

Silence.

'Ere.

Sue *takes* **Eddie**'s *cracker.*

Sue   'Ant paid nine ninety-nine f' you t' just sit there, come on. Come on, Ted.

Eddie *takes his cracker,* **Sue** *takes the other end.*

They pull – it pops.

Eddie *puts his hat on.*

Silence.

Sue   Still another ten in box.

Silence.

Yer don't have to wear that one.

Eddie   I want to wear this one.

Sue   I'm just sayin' . . .

Eddie   What?

Sue   Yer don't have to wear that one.

Eddie   It's fine.

Sue   Sat there, pullin' faces . . .

Eddie   I said it's fine.

Silence.

Sue *takes her joke.*

Sue   What did the envelope say to the stamp?

Silence.

Stick with me n' we'll go places.

Silence.

Sue *takes the joke from* **Eddie***'s cracker.*

Sue   How do snails keep their shells shiny?

Silence.

Snail polish.

Silence.

Sue *looks through the contents of her cracker.*

Oh. It's a puzzle, look.

Sue *opens the small plastic puzzle, unrolls the instructions.*

Sue *examines the instructions.*

Think yer meant to piece it together.

Sue *tries sticking the pieces together.*

Can't be right. I think this bit sticks to this bit . . .

Sue *continues.*

No. No, I don't think . . .

Sue *continues.*

Ah. That's it. There, look – it's a . . .

The toy falls apart.

It's supposed to spin. It's a spinny thing.

Eddie *takes the toy and fixes it.*

He passes it back to **Sue**.

Eddie   Spin it.

Sue   What?

Eddie   Spin it.

Sue   No need t' shout. I know what I'm doin'.

Sue *spins the toy.*

It spins.

Silence.

Sue   Bit o' fun.

Silence.

What did you get?

Sue *takes* **Eddie**'s *cracker, empties it out.*

She pulls out a plastic bracelet.

Sue   Oh now.

Sue *takes the plastic bracelet out of its wrapper.*

Now that's more like it.

Sue *puts the bracelet on.*

Look.

Silence.

They eat.

Silence.

He called.

Eddie   What?

Sue   He called.

Silence.

Nice to 'ear a friendly voice. Said there's still time if yer want to change yer mind. Still a few hours before bedtime.

Silence.

Don't worry about yer father n' me I said. Quite happy t' keep ourselves occupied for one year. Up to me eyes wi'the bloody turkey as it is. One year won't hurt.

Eddie   No.

Sue   Do as yer please, I said. Long as you're happy.

Silence.

Said yer'd give 'im a ring later. Once we're settled.

Silence.

Sue   Special on tonight.

Eddie   What?

Sue   *Only Fools n' Horses.* It's a Christmas special. Del-Boy comes up with a plan to make some money. He doesn't want anythin' to do with it, Rodney I mean. He knows it'll only spell trouble. Course 'e's right. It all goes wrong in the end.

Silence.

Looks hysterical on the advert.

Silence.

Yer will call 'im, won't yer, Ted? He'll be ever so sad if yer don't. Yer will though, won't yer?

Eddie   Yes.

Silence.

Sue   Didn't know yer liked Neil Young.

Eddie   'Oo?

Sue   The album they bought yer.

Eddie   Yes I do.

Sue   Well I didn't know. Yer've never mentioned it to me. Yer've never expressed an opinion.

Silence.

Then yer wouldn't would yer?

Eddie   No.

Sue   Not to me anyway.

Silence.

Well. He had his dinner at two and . . .

Sue *checks her watch.*

Sue   Oh. Should be there be now. Off to 'er uncle's. Her great-uncle. On 'er daddy's side. In his nineties, bless. Lives way across the other side of the city 'e said. Been there since the fifties. Bit of a convoy. All the grandkids, the whole family – must be what? Twenty, twenty-five of 'em all in all. All in their cars, over the River Thames n' back. Every year apparently. Somethin' of a tradition. Sounded very busy over the phone – Well, yer'll hear. Hardly get a word o' sense out of 'im. Says they've taken to 'im though. Even with the noise, 'e says they're all very kind.

Silence.

They've offered t' pay f' the weddng.

Eddie   What?

Sue   'Er father. He's written them a cheque.

Eddie   'Ow much?

Sue   Sounds quite the character. Just cracked open the bubbly when he called. Ten o'clock in the mornin'.

Eddie   'Ow much?

Sue   Hardly settin' an example are they?

Silence.

He didn't say.

Silence.

They've got a piano.

Eddie   Good.

Sue   Said he has to have a singalong later. Yer know what he's like. Him. Givin' it 'Jingle Bells'. Haven't heard a note out of 'im since 'e were three year old. Said yer'd better start practisin', love. Said yer'd better make the most o' that champagne while there's time. Have a brandy or two, God 'elp us.

Eddie   He'll be fine.

Sue   Course he's bound to have a few.

Eddie   Ay.

Sue   No stoppin' 'im usually.

Silence.

Under the table last year.

Eddie *chuckles.*

Sue   With his hat on.

Eddie *and* **Sue** *both chuckle.*

Sue (*chuckling*)   The bloody . . . The whatsit . . . The . . .

Eddie *laughs.*

Sue   Round his ankles . . .

Sue *laughs,* **Eddie** *laughs.*

Sue   Still got the picture.

Silence.

Eddie *and* **Sue** *eat.*

Silence.

Sue   Give what yer can though, don't yer?

Eddie   Ay.

Sue   Every little helps.

Silence.

Over the moon with his Diskman.

Eddie   What?

Sue   We sent 'im a Diskman.

Eddie   Oh.

Sue   Very thoughtful of yer. He told me t' tell yer. Over the moon.

Eddie   Right.

Sue   Take it with 'im on the tube train. Keep 'im on 'is toes. Not just compact disks neither. Tune into Radio Four if 'e wants. Five Live f' the sport. Thinkin' o' gettin' one meself.

Eddie   Make a start.

Sue   What?

Eddie   Tomorrow. Get that gate fixed up out back.

Sue   Been sayin' that f' weeks.

Eddie   Pick up some hinges.

Sue   Shops aren't open till Friday.

Eddie   Done be lunchtime.

Sue   Weather says it's goin' t' snow.

Eddie   Stop 'er gettin' ideas. Stop 'er runnin' off.

Sue   Be good t' get out the 'ouse, Ted.

Silence.

Wear it on the day, can't I?

Eddie   What?

Sue   Go well with me frock, won't it?

Eddie   Right.

Sue   Go well with me frock.

Silence.

Sue *removes the bracelet from her wrist.*

Sue *puts the bracelet back in its plastic wrapper.*

Silence.

Sue   Wouldn't want to upstage the bride though, would I?

Silence.

Sue *pours wine and drinks.*

Silence.

Sue   She's very good for 'im, though.

Eddie   Ay.

Sue   She's a very good influence, I mean. Pair of 'em together, they'll rule the bloody world time they're forty.

Eddie   If yer say so.

Sue   Quite a looker.

Eddie   What?

Sue   Said so yerself. The quiet type. Hardly get a word out of 'er on the phone. She's quite a looker, yer said.

Eddie   Did I?

Sue   Told me she looked like Catherine Zeta Jones.

Eddie   When?

Sue   Barely took yer eyes off the poor girl. Small wonder she's so shy, you gawpin'.

Silence.

Thought they might've driven up.

Eddie   Ay.

Sue   Driven up f' Boxin' Day at least.

Silence.

Scared 'er off.

Eddie   What?

Sue   I said yer must've scared 'er away.

Silence.

Sat there like Stone'enge.

Silence.

Funny.

Eddie   What is?

Sue   Hard to imagine he'd ever settle down. Take after yer father, I said to 'im. 'E were just the same when we first met. All that ambition. All that hair.

Silence.

Always thought yer'd end up shacked up in some commune, savin' the bloody . . .

Eddie *grabs the carving knife.*

Sue   What?

Eddie *carves off a turkey leg.*

Sue   Eddie . . .

Pause.

Eddie, don't.

Eddie *takes the turkey leg and puts it in the dish with the roast potatoes.*

Sue   Use the roll. The kitchen roll . . .

Eddie *removes the left-over roast potatoes and puts them on his plate.*

Sue   Grease all over the tablecloth, be careful.

Eddie *exits with the dish.*

Sue   Spoil that dog!

Silence.

Sue *fills up her glass of white wine.*

Sue *sips.*

Silence.

Sue *drinks half the glass of white wine.*

Sue *fills up her glass again.*

Sue *sips.*

Silence.

Sue *unbuttons her top.*

Sue *checks her left breast for lumps.*

Silence.

Sue *buttons up her top.*

Silence.

Sue *swallows the wine down in one.*

Silence.

Sue *gets up out of her chair.*

Sue *serves the vegetables and the turkey carcass onto* **Eddie***'s plate.*

Sue *sits.*

Silence.

Eddie *re-enters from the kitchen.*

Eddie *sits.*

Eddie *eats.*

Silence.

Sue   D'yer have to?

Silence.

Eddie *eats.*

Silence.

Sue   Don't do that, Eddie. Right in me 'car.

Silence.

Eddie *finishes eating, lays his cutlery on the plate.*

Silence.

Sue   Still some left.

Eddie   Stuffed.

Sue   Not like you. Get it eaten.

Silence.

Get it eaten, I said.

Silence.

Eddie *sparks a cigarette.*

Silence.

Sue   Mind yer don't get ash all over that.

Eddie   What?

Sue   Wunt want t' ruin it. All the trouble she's gone to.

Silence.

Should call 'im.

Silence.

Don't want t' leave it too late.

Eddie   In a minute.

Silence.

Sue   I went out.

Silence.

I went out.

Eddie   Did yer?

Sue   Next door. Poked me 'ead round the door this mornin'. Dropped off their card.

Silence.

Told 'im we'd have Brett for an hour.

Eddie   What?

Sue   Just for an hour. Thought we'd be doin' 'em a favour, bit o'peace.

Silence.

He's not all bad.

Eddie   He's a little bastard.

Sue   Liven this place up forra start.

Silence.

They've got enough to t' think about with the new baby.

Eddie   Fine.

Sue   She's only just out the hospital f' Chrissakes.

Eddie   I said it's –

Sue   Show some compassion.

Silence.

Said he could play with Lucky.

Eddie   You . . . ?

Sue   I said he could play with Lucky.

Eddie   What time?

Sue   He's comin'.

Silence.

Might not come at all. Might be fast asleep by now, yer know what they're like at that age. Day's over by six.

Silence.

Help me put the dishes away.

Silence.

Have it done in no time, the two of us.

Eddie   Ay.

Sue   She's not expectin' yer.

Eddie   What?

Sue   Pamela. She's not . . .

Eddie   No.

Sue   Give me a hand then.

Eddie   I will.

Silence.

Sue   Nobody's forcin' yer, Ted.

Silence.

Come n' go as yer please.

Silence.

Sue *pours wine and drinks.*

Silence.

Sue   Play a game later.

Silence.

Trivial Pursuits. That's a good game. You're good at general knowledge. You are. Yer better than me, I'm hopeless.

Silence.

Bit o' fun.

Silence.

Well. Think it's almost time for . . .

The phone rings.

That'll be 'im now.

Long pause.

Well, go on.

Eddie *stubs out his cigarette.*

Eddie *gets up out of his chair.*

The phone stops ringing.

Eddie *sits back down.*

Silence.

Eddie   Expect 'e'll call back later.

Sue   Expect 'e will.

Silence.

Expect 'e'll leave a message if yer give it a few . . .

Eddie   I don't love you.

Silence.

Sue   Yer entitled to yer opinion.

Silence.

Eddie   I'll do it.

Blackout.

Scene Two

Same day. 8.00 p.m.

Brett *and* **Sue** *sitting at the table.*

Brett *reluctantly eats a dish of Christmas pudding.*

Sue *sips her wine.*

They both wear Christmas-cracker hats.

Sue   How is it?

Silence.

I made it special. Yer mummy says it's yer favourite, she told me. She talks about you a lot.

Silence.

Squirty cream.

Silence.

Make yer big n' strong. Make yer burst like a balloon.

Silence.

Just a little bit then, eh?

Sue *squirts cream on to* **Brett***'s pudding.*

Sue   It is Christmas after all.

Silence.

Oh.

Sue *pulls a dog hair out of the cream.*

Sue   One of Lucky's by the look of it.

Sue *wipes the dog hair on to a napkin, then licks her fingers clean.*

Sue   Ooh. Yummy.

Silence.

Must be very exciting. Santa bring yer lots of presents. I bet 'e did. Someone's been a good boy this year. Someone's been very lucky. Little sister t' share yer stockin' with.

Brett   S'pose.

Sue   Someone to play with.

Brett *shrugs.*

Sue   Size of yer hand, int she?

Brett   Yeah.

Sue   I've seen 'er.

Silence.

Remember when you were that age. Had to look after yer one night. Yer don't remember, do yer? Still in nappies back then, practically screamed the house down. Tried puttin' you in the bath, keep yer quiet. Yer wouldn't have it. Could hear yer halfway down the street.

Silence.

Bet yer've got a fair few admirers at school now, eh? Handsome lad like you.

Brett   No.

Sue   Seen yer out the back with yer football. Proper little David Beckham. Must be havin' to fight 'em off. I bet you are. I bet they're hangin' off your shorts.

Silence.

Take after yer father.

Brett   Wanna go 'ome.

Sue   Oh now . . .

Brett   Wanna go 'ome.

Sue   Yer've only just got 'ere.

Brett   Shuddup.

Sue   What did you promise?

Brett *shrugs.*

Sue   Promised t' be good.

Silence.

Promised yer mum I'd take care of yer. She's only next door, cheer up.

Brett   Can I 'ave some Coke?

Sue   Haven't finished yer squash yet.

Brett   Mum said I could 'ave some Coke.

Sue   Everyone likes lemon squash. It's good f' yer, come on.

Brett   Tastes like pee.

Sue   What?

Brett   Nothin'.

Sue   Tastes like what?

Sue *sips the drink.*

Funny tastin' pee.

Silence.

Brett   Our tree's massive.

Sue   It is.

Brett   Yer can see ours from the park. Yours is titchy compared.

Silence.

Sue   Lovely sweater. My Danny's one just like it. When he was small like you. Stripes. He had a motorbike one year. A toy one, that is. Barry Sheen on top. Bet yer'd like one o' them. That or a racin' car.

Brett *shrugs.*

Sue   Lucky if I got an orange when I was your age. Didn't even have decorations in my house. Not with my dad. Couldn't tell if it were Christmas or Easter. Couldn't tell the difference. No one t' play with. Wouldn't like that now, would yer?

Brett   No.

Sue   Wouldn't like that at all.

Brett   Got a Gandalf.

Sue   Have yer now?

Brett   And a Gollum. They're in me drawer. They talk to each other.

Sue   Do they?

Brett *shrugs.*

Sue   Are you the Lord of the Rings?

Brett   No.

Sue   I think you are.

Brett   I'm Frodo Baggins.

Sue   What am I, then?

Brett   Nowt.

Silence.

Be a cavetroll if yer want.

Sue   Oh.

Brett   That's all that's left.

Sue   What does a cavetroll do?

Brett   Kill it.

Sue   What?

Brett   Kill yer.

Sue   Oh.

Brett   Shoot an arrow in yer gob.

Sue   Long as it's just for fun.

Brett   No.

Silence.

Sue   Sing me a carol.

Silence.

Must know a carol or two, surely. Don't they teach yer them at school? I used t' be in the choir at my school.

Silence.

Sue *sings.*

> Away in a manger,
> No crib for a bed,
> The little lord Jesus
> Laid down his sweet head.
>
> The stars in the bright sky
> Looked down where he lay,
> The little lord Jesus
> Asleep in the hay.

Brett *finishes his pudding, lays his spoon down.*

Brett   Finished now.

Sue   What d'yer say?

Brett   Thank you.

Sue   Thank you what?

Brett   Mrs Webber . . .

Sue   That's right . . .

Brett   Mrs Webber.

Sue   Good.

Brett   Mrs Webber, Mrs Webber, Mrs Webber!

Silence.

Sue   Well. Yer've done very well.

Brett   Can I play with your dog?

Sue   Oh . . .

Brett   Mum said I could play with your dog.

Sue   Afraid yer've just missed 'er, duck.

Brett   No I 'ant.

Sue   They're only round the park. Should be back in a few minutes.

Brett   But . . .

Sue   Doubt she'll be up to much playin' anyway. She's very old. Barely lift 'er out the basket once my Ted's 'ad 'is way. Be fifteen come May. That's over a hundred in dog years.

Brett   I know.

Sue   Well then.

Silence.

Play with me in the meantime, can't yer?

Silence.

So.

Silence.

How is everything? At home, I mean.

Silence.

Look under the tree, yer might find somethin' special.

Silence.

Oh.

Sue *finds a photo album on the table.*

Sue   Look what I found.

Brett   Shuddup.

Sue   Might find Lucky if we're lucky, come on.

Sue *takes the photo album and sits by* **Brett**.

She opens the album, showing **Brett** *the photographs.*

Silence.

Sue   This was her when she was just a puppy. Goin' back years. 1988. See my ankle in the shot, look.

Brett *shrugs.*

Sue   This one's even earlier. Alton Towers. That's my Danny in the queue for the corkscrew. Can't've been much older than you are now.

Silence.

That's the three of us on the log flume. Look at 'is little face, look.

Silence.

Lucky again. In the Lake District one summer.

Silence.

Danny at his sports day. He came third in the egg n' spoon.

Silence.

That's him in his Boy George phase. Pullin' one of 'is faces. Think he'd just had his TB jab.

Silence.

Lucky.

Silence.

Oh. Oh now. That's Danny in the school play. *Bugsy Malone.*
You wouldn't recognise 'im would yer? At the back there –
Can you see him?

Silence.

Him with one of his girlfriends. Don't know what ever
happened to her.

Silence.

That's him on the mornin' of his GCSE results.

Silence.

That's him on the evenin' of his GCSE results.

Silence.

Looks like Neil from *The Young Ones* here. Eyes the size of
saucers.

Silence.

That's him at the interchange in town. On his way down
to London. On his way to university. Big strong man there i'nt
'e?

Brett *shrugs.*

Sue   You'll be as tall as that one day.

Silence.

Lucky.

Silence.

Lucky in the bath.

Silence.

Don't know what this one's meant t' be.

Silence.

Lucky again. Lickin' the lens. Big fat nose, what d'yer call it?

Brett *shrugs.*

Sue   Call it 'er snout.

Silence.

Lucky with 'er dad last year. In the park.

Silence.

Lucky with an apple on 'er head. One o' my Ted's tricks, I think.

Silence.

In 'er basket, look.

Silence.

Lucky.

Silence.

Lucky again.

Silence.

Sue *flicks through the photo album.*

Silence.

Sue *puts the photo album away.*

Silence.

Sue *pours herself a glass of wine and drinks.*

Silence.

'Ave a glass of brandy if yer'd rather.

Silence.

Christmas wunt be Christmas without a drop of brandy or . . .

Brett   Gonna send me 'ome now?

Sue   Oh . . .

Brett   I'm bored.

Sue   Well, I don't think . . .

Brett   Yer borin'.

Sue   Think yer'd better keep them thoughts to yerself, don't you?

Brett   Piss off.

Silence.

Sue   Know what we do with words like that?

Brett   No.

Sue   Flush 'em down the toilet f' the rats to 'ave their way.

Silence.

Wunt want to go down with 'em.

Brett   Yeah.

Sue   Down the toilet.

Brett   Better than 'ere.

Silence.

Sue   Don't yer want t' know what Santa's got yer?

Brett   I am Santa.

Sue   Well . . .

Brett   I am.

Silence.

Sue   Yer name's on it.

Silence.

Brett *climbs out of his chair and moves to the Christmas tree.*

Brett *investigates the tree.*

Sue   Good boy.

Brett *grabs the angel off the top of the tree.*

Sue   Brett!

Brett   Where's 'er eyes gone?

Sue Yer'll break it!

Brett She 'ant got no eyes left.

Sue Never mind that!

Brett But she can't . . .

Sue Put it back!

Brett *throws the angel down.*

Sue Brett!

Brett *stamps on the angel.*

Silence.

Sue Not very nice now, was it?

Brett No.

Sue Not very nice at all.

Silence.

Well?

Silence.

Brett *picks up the angel.*

Sue Almost as old as I am, that thing.

Brett So?

Sue Only comes out once a year.

Brett Do 'er voice.

Sue No.

Brett Want to 'ear 'er voice, do 'er voice.

Sue I've already told . . .

Brett Go on.

Sue She 'ant got no voice.

Silence.

Brett *fixes the angel back on the tree.*

Sue   Good boy.

Silence.

Sue   On the tag, look.

Brett *checks the tag on the present.*

Sue   Well. This is a surprise.

Brett *unwraps the present.*

It's a Sheffield Wednesday football strip.

Sue   Ooh, I say.

Brett *investigates the strip.*

Sue   Very fancy. They are your colours, aren't they? Weren't sure if yer were Wednesday or United.

Brett   United.

Sue   Oh.

Brett   Red n' white.

Sue   Are you sure?

Brett   The Blades.

Sue   But I . . .

Brett   Stupid.

Silence.

Sue   Oh. Well, I'm sure I can always get it changed.

Brett   No yer can't.

Sue   I'm sure if I . . .

Brett   Already got one.

Sue   What?

Brett   Stupid.

Sue Now look . . .

Brett I get one every season. Wear it t' the match on Saturdays. Wayne Allison's the best, he's the chief. 'Im n' Kozluk.

Sue I see.

Brett Michael Tonge's not bad either.

Sue My Danny used t' support Sheffield Wednesday.

Brett So?

Sue He used t' go t' the games back when they were in Division One.

Brett Shithead.

Sue What?

Brett He's a shithead, then. Only shit'eads support Wednesday.

Silence.

Sue Try it on anyway, can't we?

Brett No.

Sue See if it fits.

Brett I don't . . .

Sue Come on . . .

Brett . . . want to . . .

Sue Just a second . . .

Brett Ow!

Sue Don't be such a baby . . .

Brett Geddoff . . .

Sue Brett . . .

Brett Geddoff me!

Sue   In a minute.

Brett   No.

Sue   Let's see yer first.

Brett   They're not my team!

Sue   Come on . . .

Brett   They're not my . . .!

Sue   I'll tell yer when they're yer fuckin' team or not, get it on!

Brett   But . . .

Sue *slaps* **Brett** *across the face.*

Silence.

Sue *moves to the table and sits.*

Sue *pours wine and drinks.*

Silence.

Brett *gets changed into the football strip.*

Silence.

Sue   There. Didn't hurt now, did it?

Brett   No.

Sue   Let me see.

Silence.

Well. Don't you look the bonnie prince?

Silence.

Aren't yer havin' a good time?

Brett   No.

Sue   Are you sulkin'?

Brett   No.

Sue   Are you a Grumpus McMumpus?

Silence.

I think you are.

Silence.

Wunt tell on yer Auntie Susan, would yer?

Brett *shrugs.*

Sue   Our little secret.

Brett   You started it.

Sue   What?

Brett   Yer did.

Sue   Don't be . . .

Brett   Only 'ere 'cause they sent me.

Sue   Well, if yer weren't so naughty . . .

Brett   Dint want t' come at all.

Sue   We can't always have what we want.

Brett   I dint.

Sue   Then yer'll just 'ave t' make do then, won't yer?

Brett   No.

Sue   Wunt want to upset yer mother now.

Brett   She dunt care.

Sue   Wunt want to upset 'er.

Brett   She hates your guts.

Sue   Now, don't . . .

Brett   'Er and me dad.

Sue   Don't be silly.

Brett   She does.

Sue   She doesn't hate anyone.

Brett   I 'eard 'er.

Sue   No one hates anyone, Brett, that's a fact.

Brett   Waits inside.

Sue   Sit down.

Brett   Waits f' yer to go back in when she hangs out line. Dunt like the way yer pick up me sister, she said, says it's rude. Said yer don't hold babies like that, said yer held 'er like a cat. Says she only lets yer do it 'cause yer old. 'Cause yer old n' yer stupid n' yer 'ant got none of yer own.

Silence.

Sue   More puddin' if yer want it.

Silence.

'Ave some puddin'.

Brett   No.

Sue   Just a sliver now, come on.

Brett   Can I use your toilet?

Sue   Come on, Brett.

Brett   Need a wee.

Sue   Don't play . . .

Brett   Need a . . .

Sue   . . . silly beggars with me!

Silence.

Think yer in enough trouble, don't you?

Brett   No.

Sue   Trouble at school.

Brett   Yer wrong.

Sue   Disruptin' classes. Bullyin'. Pickin' on kids half yer size.

Brett   Shuddup.

Sue   Yer mother told me all about it.

Silence.

Give some lad a nose-bleed, dint yer?

Brett   She's lyin'.

Sue   Couldn't believe it when I 'eard. That can't be right,
I said.

Brett   Weren't just me.

Sue   Must be mistaken, surely.

Brett   Marcus from two doors down, he's the one who starts
it. He does.

Silence.

Sue *refills her glass of wine.*

Sue   Well, I don't know who keeps kickin' my wheelie bin
over every mornin'. Twenty minutes it took me to clean it all
off the road last week.

Silence.

Yer wouldn't know anythin' about that now, would you?

Brett   No.

Sue   Are you sure?

Brett   Shuddup.

Sue   I can always ask yer mother.

Silence.

I'm sure she'd be very interested to hear about that.

Brett   Weren't me.

Sue   Some of us are better at keepin' secrets than others.

Brett   It wasn't.

Sue   Brett . . .

Brett   Why's it always me all the time?

Silence.

Sue   Can't help the way yer feel, poor thing.

Silence.

Sue *pours a glass of brandy and hands it to* **Brett**.

Sue   World dunt revolve round you no more.

Silence.

Brett *hesitates, then sips the brandy.*

Sue   Little baby sister t' think of. Surprised they've got the time t' play with you no more.

Silence.

Must get very lonely.

Brett   I 'ate 'er.

Sue   What?

Brett   Can't even speak.

Sue   Bet yer'd like t' give 'em all bloody nose-bleeds given the chance.

Brett   Yeah.

Sue   I know I would.

Silence.

Can hear everythin' through these walls.

Silence.

Way yer mum n' dad've been arguin' last few month, dread t' think how you must feel.

Silence.

Can't see 'em lastin' much longer, t' tell yer the truth.

Silence.

Know yer can always come to me though, don't yer?

Brett   Yeah.

Sue   Door's always open.

Brett   Yeah.

Sue   Yes what?

Brett   Mrs Webber, I know.

Silence.

Sue   'Ere.

Sue *gets out of her chair.*

She finds her handbag and takes out her purse.

From the purse **Sue** *takes out a twenty-pound note.*

She hands the note to **Brett**.

Sue   Buy yerself somethin' nice. Go on.

Brett *takes the note from* **Sue** *and pockets it.*

Sue   Make up f' the strip.

Silence.

Sue *moves to the tree and takes the angel off.*

Silence.

Sue *moves to* **Brett**, *holding the angel.*

Silence.

Sue (*as the angel*)   'Appy Christmas, Brett.

Silence.

Sue (*as the angel*)   'Appy Christmas, Brett.

Silence.

Sue *hands the angel to* **Brett**.

Sue   Keep 'er in yer bedroom with the others, can't yer?

Brett Yeah.

Sue Give 'er a name.

Brett Mrs Webber.

Sue That's a nice name.

Silence.

Come 'ere.

Brett What?

Sue Come 'ere. Come on.

Silence.

See? That's better int it?

Silence.

Must be tired, poor thing.

Silence.

Expect they'll be wonderin' where yer've got to.

Silence.

Sleep in my Danny's old room if yer'd rather.

Brett Yeah.

Sue Still got all 'is old England posters on the walls. Might be some players yer recognise.

Silence.

Nip across. Tell 'em how yer feel. Tell 'em yer'd rather stay at yer auntie's, get out from under their feet. Sit in front the telly, couldn't we? Find some cartoons t' watch. Yer'd like that, wunt yer? Bit o' peace. Time t' think.

Silence.

Christ was born on this day.

Silence.

Ask f' yer pyjamas. Any toys yer might want.

Brett   Paint 'er some new ones.

Sue   What?

Brett   Felt tips in me drawer. Paint 'er some new eyes, can't we? Paint 'er some new ones so she can see.

Blackout.

Scene Three

Same day. Midnight.

Eddie *sitting in the armchair, watching television.*

On his lap is a basket of nuts. Using a nutcracker, he eats the nuts.

He swigs from a bottle of beer.

He has a black eye.

Silence.

Sue *enters in her nightie, carrying a quilt, sheets and a pillow.*

Sue   Put 'im in your room. Won't hurt for one night.

She proceeds to make **Eddie**'s *makeshift bed.*

Sue   Don't know what yer do t' get it in such a state. Found six o' my good coffee cups in there just now. Ashtrays tipped over the floor.

Silence.

Even Danny used t' know when to use the Hoover when he had to.

Silence.

Small wonder yer never get any sleep wi' these sheets. Should put 'em in the bathroom like I asked.

Silence.

This alright for yer?

Eddie   Ay.

Sue   Always grab a towel from out the airin' cupboard.

Silence.

Must be shattered.

Eddie   I am.

Sue   Yer look it.

Silence.

Like t' get an early start. Busy day ahead of us. Said we'd take him along if he wants. He's never been out in Derbyshire before. Thought we might take him over Snake Pass. Long as the car 'olds up. Long as it's not too . . .

Eddie *throws a nut at* **Sue**.

Sue   Eddie . . .

Eddie *throws a nut at* **Sue**.

Sue   Don't do that.

Eddie *throws a nut at* **Sue**.

Sue   Don't do that, Eddie.

Eddie *eats.*

Silence.

Sue *picks up the nuts.*

Sue *puts them back in the basket.*

Silence.

Should take a peek.

Eddie   I'm watchin'.

Sue   Out like a light once 'is 'ead 'it the pillow. Sweetest little thing. Takes yer right back.

Silence.

Take a little peek, Ted, come on.

Eddie   Yer hair's fallin' out.

Sue   What?

Eddie   I've noticed.

Silence.

Sue   Oh. Carry on.

Eddie   Up Khyber.

Sue   What?

Eddie   *Carry On Up Khyber.*

Sue   Don't raise your voice at me.

Eddie   Shift.

Sue   There's children asleep, fast asleep . . .

Eddie   Fat arse blockin' the sun.

Sue   Turn it down.

Eddie   Yer blockin' the screen!

Sue   The remote, Ted.

Sue *takes the remote and turns the sound down.*

Sue   Give 'im bloody nightmares wi' that racket.

Silence.

Eddie *flicks channels.*

Silence.

Eddie *eats.*

Silence.

Sue   *Spartacus.*

Eddie   Ay.

Silence.

Sue   Eddie.

Silence.

Eddie . . .

Eddie   What?

Sue   Gone midnight already.

Silence.

Can I watch?

Eddie   If yer must.

Sue   Thought we might keep each other company.

Silence.

Sleep in my room if yer'd rather.

Silence.

Moved it all round last week. Put the bed under the window. Lovely in the mornings with the light shinin' through.

Silence.

Very good, int 'e?

Eddie   What?

Sue   Tony Curtis.

Eddie   'Oo?

Sue   He's very underrated, they say.

Silence.

Fetch the little portable up from the kitchen. Use the extension cable. Sure I can find some room for it on the dresser. Keep each other warm.

Silence.

Yer can smoke.

Eddie   What?

Sue   Open the window a bit. Keep the heatin' on, well . . . Hardly tell the difference, will we?

Eddie   No.

Sue   I don't mind.

Eddie   Thanks.

Sue   Have the fright of his life, 'e finds yer down 'ere in the mornin'. Sprawled out like that. What's 'e goin' t' think, eh?

Eddie *takes a cigarette from his packet.*

Sue   What's he goin' t' think, Ted?

Silence.

Well?

Eddie   Let 'im think.

Sue   Don't be like that.

Eddie   Leave me alone.

Sue   Eddie . . .

Eddie   Move!

Sue   I've asked you once already . . .

Eddie   Jesus Christ . . .

Sue   Are you comin' t' bed?

Silence.

Eddie *lights the cigarette.*

Silence.

Sue   Want t' watch that, you. Bedbound time yer sixty, way yer carry on. End up like yer father, bloody great hole through yer throat.

Silence.

Don't say I didn't warn yer.

Silence.

Know 'ow restless she gets without 'er dad.

Eddie   What?

Sue   Lucky.

Silence.

Come upstairs with us, can't she? Let 'er sleep on the bed for once. Can't imagine there's much life in 'er now. Not after your carry on.

Eddie   Sue, please . . .

Sue   Has she even had 'er supper?

Silence.

Ted.

Eddie   What?

Sue   Where is she?

Silence.

The dog, where's the dog?

Silence.

Yer dint leave the gate open did yer?

Eddie   No.

Sue   Where is she?

Eddie   Go to bed.

Sue   She can't just vanish.

Eddie   She's fine.

Sue   She can't just vanish, Ted.

Eddie   I paid for 'er!

Sue   But . . .

Eddie   She's mine!

Silence.

Eddie *stubs out the cigarette.*

Silence.

Sue   Yer left 'er there.

Eddie   Yes.

Sue   Yer left 'er there.

Silence.

Yer know she dunt like bein' left without 'er basket.

Silence.

Yer know what she's like, Ted, she'll go frantic by 'erself. Leave 'er stranded. Some bloody stranger . . .

Eddie   She's not.

Sue   That's exactly what she is!

Silence.

Eddie   Pamela.

Sue   Fine.

Eddie   'Er name's Pamela.

Sue   Gone all bloody night.

Eddie   It's over.

Sue   What?

Eddie   It's finished.

Sue   What's she done t' yer?

Eddie   Sue . . .

Sue   Yer eye.

Eddie   Let go.

Sue   Above yer eye –

Eddie   Leave it.

Sue   Yer've been fightin'.

Eddie   I knocked it.

Sue   You . . .

Eddie   On the door.

Sue   Which door?

Eddie   Her front door.

Sue   As yer were leavin'?

Eddie   As I was leavin', yes.

Eddie *tries to turn the volume up, using the remote.*

Sue *snatches the remote from his hand and turns the telly off.*

Sue   More of a scratch than a knock.

Eddie   Give it back.

Sue   Couldn't see where you were goin'.

Eddie   No.

Sue   Yer couldn't see.

Eddie   It's possible.

Sue   Yer drunk.

Eddie   . . .

Sue   Yer not drunk. Yer couldn't see where yer were goin'.

Eddie   Look . . .

Sue   Keep secrets from me.

Eddie   I already told . . .

Sue   Yer've tried it on with 'er, 'ant yer?

Eddie *goes to take a nut.*

Sue *knocks the basket of nuts out of his lap.*

Silence.

Sue   Mark o' bleedin' Zorro.

Silence.

Sue *gets down on the ground and picks up the nuts one by one, putting them in the basket.*

Silence.

Sue   Wunt be seen dead with the likes o' you.

Eddie   No.

Sue   Woman like 'er.

Silence.

Missed that chance years ago.

Eddie   Sue . . .

Sue   I'm not a bloody fool!

Sue *puts the last of the nuts back in the basket.*

Sue *hands the basket back to* **Eddie**.

Silence.

Sue *moves to the table and pours herself a glass of wine.*

She drinks.

Silence.

Sue   Don't suppose she's had any word?

Eddie   What?

Sue   That husband of hers.

Eddie   No.

Sue   Don't suppose there's any chance . . .

Eddie   She's sellin' up.

Sue   What?

Eddie Lookin' at some villa.

Sue What?

Eddie Spanish villa.

Silence.

On the internet.

Sue Oh.

Eddie Reckons she can get work over there.

Sue Tried t' talk 'er out of it, did yer?

Silence.

Yer know what she's like, Ted.

Silence.

Been the same since we were teenagers, it won't last. Different bloody story every month, you know that.

Silence.

Might want t' put some TCP on that. Stop it swellin'.

Silence.

Do 'er good. Bit o' sunshine.

Eddie Ay.

Sue Damn sight cheaper than over 'ere. Wouldn't say no meself.

Silence.

Can't remember the last time we had an 'oliday.

Silence.

Eddie.

Silence.

Eddie . . .

Eddie I'm not cryin'.

Silence.

Sue   Come to bed.

Silence.

Just tonight, Ted, please. Come to bed.

Silence.

Sue *moves to the table and sits.*

She pours and drinks more wine.

Silence.

Read any good books?

Silence.

Eddie . . .

Eddie   What?

Sue   'Ant seen any in the bathroom. Thought yer might . . .

Eddie   No.

Sue   I'm readin' somethin'.

Silence.

Ian McEwan. *The Child in Time.*

Silence.

I'm re-readin' it.

Eddie   Oh.

Silence.

Sue   Thought yer might o' dipped into that Sinatra. One
'e got yer f' yer birthday.

Eddie   No.

Sue   Thought yer might've made a start.

Silence.

Been watchin' the news at all?

Silence.

Good t' know they caught 'im. Good t' see 'em steppin' up the pressure. I think it's good.

Silence.

What do you think?

Silence.

There's a Turkish couple taken over the newsagent's up the road. They're very pleasant.

Silence.

Have yer met them yet?

Silence.

Back at work on Friday.

Silence.

Go in early.

Silence.

Danny's been on the phone again. Couple o' times. Told 'im yer were flat out on the brandy. There's no wakin' 'im, I said.

Silence.

He's expectin' yer t' call. Least, 'e was. Got any sense, he'll be in bed by now. They're havin' another outin' tomorrow. She's takin' 'im to 'er mum's in Wiltshire. Show him the stables.

Silence.

She's got a bloody stables. Wants to get him saddled up on one of 'er horses. In this weather.

Silence.

Spoilt cow.

Silence.

Not the type though, is she? They've never mentioned it.

Silence.

Children.

Silence.

Should never 'ave moved down there in the first place. Should never have let 'im go, Ted.

Silence.

Course she'll leave 'im.

Silence.

He'll get cancer.

Silence.

He'll get cancer and she'll leave him.

Silence.

This time next year. The three of us.

Silence.

Number's on side.

Silence.

He's waitin' forra phone call, Ted.

Silence.

Eddie *digs into his pocket.*

Eddie *takes out a small wrapped present.*

Eddie *unwraps the present.*

A jewellery case.

Eddie *opens the jewellery case.*

Silence.

Sue   Eddie . . .

Eddie   Turn the light off.

Sue   Look at me.

Eddie   Turn out the . . .

Sue   Look at me, Ted.

Silence.

Be up for retirement in a few year.

Silence.

Take 'er the vet's.

Eddie   What?

Sue   Tell 'em she's sick. Tell 'em she's not been eatin'.

Silence.

Only take a few minutes. Won't feel a thing.

Silence.

Bury 'er in the garden.

Silence.

Yer can't go back there.

Eddie   What?

Sue   Yer goin' back there.

Silence.

Well, go on!

Eddie   Does it look like I'm . . . ?

Sue   Bended bloody knees!

Eddie   I'm not goin' anywhere, Sue.

Silence.

Sue   Bastard.

Eddie   Ay.

Sue   Careless bastard, waste my . . .

The phone rings.

Silence.

Pick it up.

Silence.

Talk to 'im.

Silence.

Talk to 'im, go on.

Silence.

Your fuckin' child, Eddie Webber, pick up the phone!

The phone stops ringing.

Long silence.

Sue *growls at* **Eddie**.

Sue *snarls at* **Eddie**.

Sue *circles* **Eddie**, *growling and snarling.*

Sue *barks at* **Eddie**.

Sue *growls and snarls and barks at* **Eddie**.

Silence.

Sue *sits at the table.*

She tries to pour more wine. There is only a trickle.

Silence.

Eddie *takes the necklace out of the case.*

Eddie *moves to* **Sue**.

Eddie *ties the necklace round* **Sue**'s *neck.*

Silence.

Eddie   Take it off.

Silence.

Yer nightie. Let me see yer.

Silence.

Eddie *returns to the armchair.*

Silence.

Eddie *takes off his shirt.*

Eddie *takes off his shoes.*

Eddie *takes off his trousers.*

Eddie *climbs into his bed.*

Silence.

Brett *enters, in his pyjamas. He holds the angel.*

Silence.

Brett   Can't sleep.

Silence.

Can't sleep.

Silence.

Brett *tugs at* **Sue**'s *arm.*

Brett   Can't sleep, I 'eard noises.

Blackout.

Scene Four

One year later.

A beach in Fuerteventura, the Canary Islands. Christmas Day.

Bright and sunny.

Two sunbeds and a beach umbrella.

Sue *lies on her front on the sunbed in her swimming costume.*

Silence.

Sue *turns over on to her back.*

She shuts her eyes.

Silence.

Sue *covers her eyes from the light.*

Silence.

Sue *opens her eyes, slowly sits up.*

Sue *looks and finds the bottle of sunlotion.*

Sue *squirts the sunlotion and rubs it into her arms.*

Silence.

Sue *gets up and moves to the beach umbrella.*

Sue *tries to put the beach umbrella up . . .*

She can't.

Sue *tries again to put the beach umbrella up . . .*

She can't.

Silence.

Sue *lies back down on the sunbed, on her front.*

Scene Five

A short time later.

The beach umbrella is up.

Eddie *and* **Sue** *lie on their backs on the sunbeds.*

Eddie *is wet from the sea, with a towel over his legs.*

Silence.

Sue   Felt that breeze.

Eddie   What?

Sue   The breeze.

Silence.

Sue   There.

Eddie   What?

Sue   Didn't yer feel it?

Eddie   No.

Sue   It came back again.

Silence.

Don't fancy that dinner tonight, d' yer?

Eddie   Ay.

Sue   Turkey roast for three hundred guests. Dunt bear thinkin' about.

Silence.

Passed that place last night. In the old town.

Eddie   If yer want.

Sue   Looked good from the outside.

Silence.

Open our presents, can't we? Take 'em with us.

Silence.

Swim far?

Eddie   What?

Sue   Did yer swim very far?

Eddie   Not really.

Sue   Couldn't see yer.

Eddie   T' the edge n' back.

Sue   That's nice.

Scene Six

A short time later.

Eddie *rubs suntan lotion on to* **Sue***'s back.*

Sue   Make sure yer do me shoulders.

Eddie   Plastered with the stuff.

Sue   What?

Eddie   Yer plastered.

Silence.

Sue   Not there.

Eddie   What?

Sue   Left a bit.

Silence.

Up a bit.

Eddie   How's that?

Sue   More. Squirt some more on.

Eddie *gently pulls the straps from* **Sue***'s shoulders.*

Eddie *squirts lotion in his palms.*

Eddie *rubs lotion on* **Sue***'s shoulders.*

Sue   That's it.

Scene Seven

A short time later.

Sue *and* **Eddie** *sitting up on their sunbeds.*

They both drink from bottles of fizzy orange pop, using straws.

Cliff Richard's 'Mistletoe and Wine' can be heard in the distance.

Silence.

Sue   Can you 'ear that?

Pause.

It's Cliff.

Eddie   What?

Sue   They're playin' bloody Cliff.

Silence.

Eddie   Someone's idea of a joke.

Sue   Bit o' fun.

Silence.

She would've loved it 'ere.

Eddie   What?

Sue   All this space.

Silence.

Sue *lies down on her sunbed.*

Silence.

Eddie *finds his cigarettes.*

He takes one out of the pack and lights it.

Sue   Very strong them, Ted.

Scene Eight

A short time later.

Sue *sunbathing, alone.*

A young boy is flying a kite.

Silence.

Sue *sits up.*

Silence.

Sue *watches the young boy.*

Silence.

Sue *lies back down.*

Scene Nine

A short time later.

Eddie *and* **Sue** *sunbathing.*

Silence.

Eddie   Not of the same calibre now.

Sue   Who?

Silence.

Who isn't? – What?

Silence.

Sue   Who?

Silence.

Did you say somethin'?

Eddie   Ronnie O'Sullivan.

Sue   What about 'im?

Silence.

Eddie   Cliff Thorburn.

Sue   What?

Eddie   Ray Reardon.

Silence.

'Urricane 'Iggins.

Silence.

Fat bloke, Canadian.

Silence.

Jimmy White.

Silence.

Went t' see it, dint we?

Sue   'Oo?

Eddie   Steve Davis.

Sue   Oh.

Eddie   Went the semi-final.

Scene Ten

A short time later.

Eddie *sunbathing.*

Sue *sitting on the edge of the sunbed, dusting down her flip-flops.*

Silence.

Sue   You alright?

Silence.

Sue *puts on her flip-flops.*

Sue   Goin' forra paddle.

Sue *pulls herself to her feet.*

Won't be long.

Sue *takes her sarong.*

Eddie *sits up.*

Sue *ties the sarong round her waist.*

Silence.

Eddie   Don't go too far.

Blackout.

The Early Bird

The Early Bird was first performed at the Queen's Theatre, Belfast, as part of the Belfast Theatre Festival, on 19 October 2006. The cast was as follows:

Debbie   Abigail McGibbon
Jack   Colm Gormley

Directed by Rachel O'Riordan
Designed by Gary McCann
Lighting by James Whiteside
Sound by James Kennedy

Characters

Debbie
Jack

Setting

Feel free to play with the setting and the physicality as pleases you, but do keep the rhythm of the speech.

'La Isla Bonita' is a Madonna song and can be found on *The Immaculate Collection* album.

Long pause.

Debbie   She left for school as normal.

Pause.

Has her breakfast. Coco Pops. Glass of milk.

Pause.

Watch her from the front window. Turns the corner on her way to the bus stop.

Pause.

Must've been what? Twenty past.

Jack   Quarter to.

Debbie   What?

Jack   Quarter to nine.

Debbie   Oh . . .

Jack   She was late.

Debbie   I was running late.

Jack   Right.

Debbie   The clock's gone forward. I forgot to set the . . . the . . .

Pause.

The thing.

Jack   What?

Debbie   I forgot to set the . . .

Pause.

Only realise once I turn on the news. Of course there was no news. Not at that time. What's the one?

Jack   What?

Debbie   What's it called? You know the one, what is it?

Jack   What?

Debbie   The programme. Straight after the news.

Jack   I wouldn't know.

Debbie   You'd left already.

Pause.

You'd left already.

Jack   I was in a rush.

Debbie   You had an early start, that's right. That's what I thought, anyway. 'He's got off early,' I thought. 'Someone's got the wind in his sails.'

Jack   You weren't thinking.

Debbie   No.

Jack   You were carrying on as normal.

Debbie   She has her breakfast, I turn on the news.

Pause.

Jack   What's she wearing?

Pause.

Debbie *and* **Jack**   What's she wearing?

Pause.

Jack   Debbie . . .

Debbie   'Bargain Hunt'.

Jack   What?

Debbie   The programme. 'Bargain Hunt', I remember now. She's got on her little orange mac. With the hood pulled up. Turns the corner and goes to catch the bus. 'Course all the other kids have left by now. I gave her a note to pass on to her teacher. I was going to ring, but . . . but I was late myself, I wasn't . . .

Pause.

You don't think, do you?

Pause.

You don't think anything's going to happen.

Jack   She'd been restless.

Debbie   What?

Jack   Come to think of it. Thinking back.

Pause.

She hadn't been herself.

Debbie   I wouldn't say that.

Pause.

I wouldn't.

Pause.

No different to any girl her age. Growing up. That age.

Jack   You think it's all part of . . .

Debbie   Growing up, that's what I said.

Jack   You think.

Debbie   What?

Jack   *You* think.

Pause.

Debbie   Jack. My partner, Jack. He thought she'd been restless.

Jack   It's the little things you notice.

Debbie   He says that now.

Jack   The little things.

Debbie   You say that now.

Jack   She's put on weight.

Debbie   You see.

Jack   She can barely fit into her own clothes.

Debbie   Oh . . .

Jack   The junk you feed her. Mars bars and fucking Monster Munch.

Debbie   So it's my fault?

Pause.

Jack   She was distant.

Debbie   Oh . . .

Jack   Reclusive.

Debbie   Come on, Jack . . .

Jack   She was.

Debbie   Like any girl that age. Growing up.

Long pause.

Of course, it'd be different had she been a boy. Maybe she would have been more . . .

Jack   Outgoing.

Debbie   Maybe.

Jack   Maybe so.

Debbie   With you at least.

Pause.

With her father.

Jack   Fine.

Debbie   With him.

Long pause.

What we're saying . . .

Pause.

What we're trying to say . . .

Jack   Maybe there was and maybe there wasn't.

Debbie   It wasn't . . .

Jack   Something.

Debbie   . . . anything either of us had really . . .

Jack   Something else going on.

Debbie   She would have told us.

Pause.

She would have told me at least.

Jack   You can't help but think the worst.

Debbie   She hadn't been picked on or anything.

Jack   We don't know that.

Debbie   She kept herself to herself.

Jack   We can't be sure of anything now.

Debbie   She's a good girl.

Jack   Right.

Debbie   An angel.

Long pause.

Jack   Debbie.

Pause.

Debbie . . .

Debbie   At least she never said.

Jack   Should I go and check on her?

Debbie   At least.

Pause.

At least she never said anything to my face.

Jack   Debbie . . .

Debbie   You don't just disappear.

Jack   Should I see that she's all right?

Debbie   You don't vanish into thin air.

Pause.

Well, do you?

Jack   No.

Debbie   Well, do you, Jack?

Long pause.

She wakes up the following morning and . . .

Jack   I'm running late.

Debbie   Have you seen her gym bag?

Jack   Debbie, please . . .

Debbie   I left it by the settee last night.

Jack   I haven't seen it.

Debbie   Are you sure you didn't move it?

Jack   Debbie . . .

Debbie   You were the last one to bed.

Jack   For Christ's sake, will you get out of my way?

Debbie   She's going to be late already.

Jack   I didn't even know she had a fucking gym bag!

Debbie   Jack . . .

Jack   Gym bag.

Debbie   Jack, don't . . .

Jack   How many bags does she need, for fucksake?

Debbie   Don't swear in front of her.

Jack   Jesus Christ . . .

Debbie   Don't swear, I said!

Jack   I don't have time for this, Deborah.

Debbie   Frighten the poor girl.

Jack   Will you . . . ?

Debbie   She's hardly touched her Coco Pops, look.

Jack   Oh now . . .

Debbie   Look at her.

Jack   Will you let me get my coat at least?

Debbie   Jack . . .

Jack   Stood there like the fucking Andes.

Debbie   Don't . . .

Jack   The pair of you.

Debbie   Don't speak to me like that.

Jack   Have you seen the time already?!

Debbie   Jack . . .

Jack   Fucking useless, what are you?!

Pause.

Well?!

Pause.

Fucking useless.

Debbie   The thing.

Jack   What?

Debbie   The thing, I forgot to set the . . .

Pause.

The . . .

Pause.

The thing, the . . .

Pause.

The programme, straight after the news. I remember because I changed the channel, I changed the channel. We have a box now, don't we?

Jack   We do.

Debbie   There's what, about a hundred fucking channels on the thing?

Jack   Right.

Debbie   I mean, it's mostly old crap, we don't . . .

Jack   Repeats.

Debbie   We don't really . . .

Jack   We don't really care for it too much.

Debbie   He likes the sport.

Jack   Sky Sports. For the cricket.

Debbie   Sorry, I don't mean to swear, I . . .

Jack   The test match.

Debbie   I don't normally . . .

Jack   The Ashes.

Debbie   It's not something I normally do. Not while she's . . .

Jack   Though I can't say I'm too fussy, you know? Boxing, the footy, golf. The beach fucking volleyball – if you get my meaning, boys.

Debbie   She's on her way out the door, and I go to call for her – I mean, she's worse than I am for forgetting what she . . .

Pause.

I'm late myself, but . . .

Pause.

But, you know?

Pause.

It can just suck you in though, can't it? The channels, I mean.

Pause.

They suck you in.

Long pause.

'Bargain Hunt'.

Pause.

'Doctors'.

Pause.

'A Place in the Sun'.

Pause.

'A Place in the Sun'.

Jack   Debbie . . .

Debbie   You remember?

Jack   Look . . .

Debbie   You remember, Jack?

Pause. She sings the chorus of 'La Isla Bonita', pausing between the first four lines and the second four lines.

Long pause.

Jack   You should call her friends.

Debbie   What?

Jack   Her friends.

Pause.

You should see if anyone's seen her.

Debbie   I don't have their numbers.

Jack   Have you checked upstairs?

Debbie   I don't . . .

Jack   Have you checked her room?

Pause.

Deborah.

Pause.

Have you looked through her drawer?

Pause.

Her things.

Debbie   What things?

Jack   Perhaps she kept a diary. Most girls her age . . .

Pause.

Check her drawer.

Debbie   No.

Jack   She might have left something.

Debbie   No, I'm thinking.

Jack   A clue, she might've written something down in her schoolwork.

Debbie   No, it wasn't. It wasn't raining, I mean. Not first thing anyway. She must've worn her blazer. Her blazer and her scarf – that's right.

Jack   Debbie . . .

Debbie   That's right. She took her blazer and her scarf, and I told her to take her umbrella.

Jack   Should I go and look for it myself?

Pause.

Debbie.

Pause.

Debbie.

Long pause.

Are you going to just fucking sit there?!

Long pause.

Debbie   Of course he's quite the temper on him.

Jack   Debbie, please . . .

Debbie   Not that you'd know it, just to look at him.

Jack   We can't . . .

Debbie   Quite the temper.

Jack   All right . . .

Debbie   Quite the man.

Jack   All right, that's . . .

Debbie   Quite the man about town.

Pause.

Not that you'd ever suspect, of course.

Jack   Deborah . . .

Debbie   Not from him, oh no.

Jack   Look . . .

Debbie   It's not in his nature.

Jack   Turn it off.

Debbie   Not with all he's achieved.

Jack   Give me the remote.

Debbie   And at such a young age.

Jack   We'll never get any sleep if you carry on . . .

Debbie   Coming home from work with his angel all gone.

Jack   She's not sleeping, Debbie.

Debbie   His angel all gone.

Long pause.

Jack   I should call them myself.

Debbie   He says.

Jack   She must have kept a diary. Most girls her age . . .

Pause.

Debbie   What?

Jack   What?

Debbie   Most girls what?

Long pause.

Jack   There must be something, there must be . . .

Pause.

Something, some . . .

Debbie   A clue.

Jack   Right.

Debbie   Something she was keeping from you.

Jack   From us.

Debbie   Some secret you made her promise . . .

Jack   Debbie, please . . .

Debbie   Something you made her . . . .

Jack   Will you let me get my coat at least?

Debbie   Jack . . .

Jack   Stood there like the fucking Andes.

Debbie   Don't . . .

Jack   The pair of you.

Debbie   Don't speak to me like that.

Jack   Have you seen the time already?!

Debbie   Jack . . .

Jack   Fucking useless, what are you?!

Pause.

Well?!

Pause.

Fucking useless.

Debbie   Come on now, girl, let's have you on your way.

Jack   I swear to God you do it on purpose.

Debbie   Let's put your little coat on now.

Jack   Debbie . . .

Debbie   Pull your hood up.

Jack   Don't ignore me!

Debbie   Yes, I know you don't want to, but . . .

Jack   Debbie!

Debbie   You're going to get yourself soaked.

Jack   Did you do it on purpose?

Debbie   Please, Kimberly, don't . . .

Jack   Answer me!

Debbie   That's it, and your umbrella now.

Jack   If you don't give me a straight answer . . .

Debbie   Hold it.

Jack   Debbie . . .

Debbie   Hold it. Like this. Hold the umbrella like this. In your hand.

Jack   It's not raining.

Debbie   The weatherman said . . .

Jack   The weatherman.

Debbie   The weatherman said it's going to rain today.

Jack   You'll believe anything.

Debbie   She's going to get herself soaked like this, now . . .

Jack   Let her go.

Debbie   Kimberly.

Jack   If she doesn't want to . . .

Debbie   Look at me.

Jack   You can't . . .

Debbie   Turn around.

Jack   Jesus Christ . . .

Debbie   Tell her.

Jack   What?

Debbie   Listen to your father.

Jack   It's late enough already.

Debbie   Tell her.

Jack   Leave the girl alone.

Debbie   Tell her.

Jack   I don't have . . .

Debbie   Tell her, Jack!

Long pause.

I told you to take the umbrella.

Pause.

Kimberly.

Jack   No.

Debbie   What?

Pause.

What did you just say?

Pause.

Just in case now, come on.

Jack   I don't want to.

Debbie   Oh . . .

Jack   I don't want to.

Debbie   Now you're just being . . .

Jack   Don't make me, Mammy, please.

Debbie   Put it in your bag at least.

Jack   But . . .

Debbie   Give me your bag.

Jack   No, please . . .

Debbie   It hardly weighs a thing now, come on.

Pause.

Come on, come here.

Pause.

What have I told you?

Pause.

Hm?

Pause.

The early bird catches what?

Pause.

What does he catch? – Don't look at the floor.

Pause.

The early bird catches what?

Jack   The worm.

Debbie   What?

Jack   The worm.

Debbie   The what worm?

Jack   The wiggly.

Debbie   The wiggly what?

Pause.

The wiggly what now?

Beat.

The wiggly what?

Jack *giggles.*

Debbie   Come on, you just said so – The wiggly . . . ?

Jack (*giggles*)   No, don't . . .

Debbie   The wiggly . . .

Jack (*giggles*)   The wiggly worm.

Debbie   What?

Jack (*giggles*)   Please . . .

Debbie   I can't hear you.

Jack (*laughing*)   Stop!

Debbie   I can't hear . . .

Jack (*laughing*)   Don't tickle me, please!

Debbie   The wiggly what?

Jack (*laughing*)   The worm, the wiggly worm!

Debbie   Who's a wiggly?

Jack (*laughing*)   Mammy, please!

Debbie   Who's a wiggly worm?

Jack (*laughing*)   Stop it, please!!

Both laughing.

Pause.

Debbie   Go on now, there's a good girl.

Pause.

You don't want to disappoint Mrs Stephens.

Pause.

Kimberly.

Pause.

You don't want to upset your father now, do you?

Pause.

Well?

Pause.

You don't want to upset anyone.

Pause.

Kimberly.

Pause.

Kimberly, please . . .

Jack   Take your clothes off.

Debbie   Kimberly . . .

Jack   Take your clothes off, come on.

Pause.

It's freezing cold, come to bed.

Pause.

Come on now, Kimberly love, it's way past your bedtime.

Debbie   But . . .

Jack   No buts, come on.

Debbie   But Daddy . . .

Jack   Daddy nothing – bed.

Debbie   But I'm not tired, Daddy.

Jack   You've got a big day ahead of you tomorrow, now come on, snuggle up, there's a good girl.

Debbie   Sleepy.

Jack   What?

Debbie   I'm not sleepy.

Jack   Of course you're sleepy, you're a sleepy-socks, we all know that.

Debbie   Daddy, please . . .

Jack   You're fighting the sleep because you're excited.

Debbie   No.

Jack   You're nervous about the big day, poor thing.

Debbie   But I'm . . .

Jack   Pull the covers up, there's a good girl.

Debbie   Can I keep the light on?

Jack   You can have anything you want, my love, you know that.

Debbie   Can I sleep in your room?

Jack   No.

Debbie   Oh . . .

Jack   I might read you a story, if you'd like.

Pause.

Would you like that?

Debbie   Yes, Daddy.

Jack   You'd like that, wouldn't you?

Debbie   Yes . . .

Jack   So long as you're good now. So long as you stay in bed and stop bothering your mammy and me.

Debbie   But . . .

Jack   No more noise.

Debbie   I heard shouting.

Jack   That's just the television. Your mammy's TV.

Debbie   Oh . . .

Jack   You shouldn't let that bother you – now, go to sleep.

Debbie   But I heard you . . .

Jack   Go to sleep.

Debbie   Daddy, please . . .

Jack   You were having nightmares, that's all.

Pause.

Tell the truth now.

Debbie   But . . .

Jack   You were having nightmares and they woke you up.

Pause.

Tell the truth now.

Debbie   I'll try, Daddy.

Jack The monsters.

Debbie Yes . . .

Jack The grizzly old monsters with their eyes bursting out their heads. They were climbing up the wall outside, weren't they?

Pause.

Kimberly . . .

Debbie Yes . . .

Jack They were tapping at the window.

Debbie They were, Daddy, yes.

Jack They were scraping their nails against the glass and you could see their faces behind the curtains.

Pause.

Well, couldn't you?

Pause.

Kimberly . . .

Debbie Daddy, please . . .

Jack You could see them, couldn't you?

Debbie But . . .

Jack You could smell them.

Debbie Yes, Daddy.

Jack There's small wonder you can't sleep. Little darling, scared to death.

Debbie I think I saw them.

Jack You think.

Debbie I think . . .

Jack They're only nightmares, come on.

Pause.

They're bad dreams.

Debbie   But I . . .

Jack   There's no one coming to get you.

Debbie   I heard you.

Jack   There's no such thing as monsters.

Debbie   But . . .

Jack   There's no such thing as monsters.

Long pause.

Would you like the story about Jesus?

Pause.

Kimberly.

Pause.

Jesus kills all the monsters. You know that, don't you?

Long pause.

What story would you like?

Pause.

Kimberly.

Pause.

Kimberly, love . . .

Debbie   Of course, the nights are getting darker.

Jack   This is true.

Debbie   You lose an hour.

Jack   Lost.

Debbie   What?

Jack   Just like that.

Pause.

Away with the fairies.

Debbie   The days and nights are getting darker.

Jack   Right.

Debbie   She turns the corner of the street to the bus stop.
She turns the corner of the street, I change the channels.
Though I'm only watching with half an eye, mind. She joins
her friends at the bus stop. There's Peggy and little Rachel.
And there's Richard, look. They're calling over to her as she
dashes across the street. She has her umbrella now . . .

Jack   She's not alone.

Debbie   No, they're jealous.

Jack   They're her friends.

Debbie   They're her jealous friends.

Pause.

Jealous bastards.

Pause.

Fucking animals.

Long pause.

Jack . . .

Jack   She has her umbrella and she joins them under the
shelter.

Pause.

She has her umbrella and she . . .

Debbie   No, she's alone, you're right.

Pause.

She's frightened.

Pause.

She's frightened of the dark.

Pause.

She's an angel.

Pause.

She's lit up like a beacon in the dark. She's got on her little orange mac with the hood pulled up.

Pause.

She's got on her blazer and her scarf, and I . . .

Pause.

She's with her friends.

Pause.

No.

Pause.

No, she . . .

Jack   Perhaps she's with them now.

Pause.

Her friends.

Debbie   Who?

Jack   Her good friends.

Debbie   Fucking animals.

Jack   Oh, come on, Deborah . . .

Debbie   The dirty beasts.

Jack   She's the one . . .

Debbie   She's an angel.

Jack   The junk you feed her, there's little wonder . . .

Debbie   I don't have their numbers, I told you.

Jack   Debbie . . .

Debbie   I don't.

Long pause.

She turns the corner and meets them. Her good, kind friends. Of course she's not alone. We're not the only ones to forget the . . .

Pause.

The thing, the . . .

Jack   The event itself is not unusual.

Debbie   Thank you, she's not – We're not, I mean . . . My partner and I.

Jack   It's an easy mistake to make.

Debbie   If there was any reason to believe . . .

Jack   To believe.

Debbie   Otherwise, I mean.

Jack   If we thought for any reason . . .

Debbie   She loves us.

Pause.

She loves us both so much. From the bottom of her tiny heart.

Pause.

We brought her into this world.

Pause.

We brought her in, Jack.

Long pause.

As before, she sings the chorus of 'La Isla Bonita'. **Jack** *joins in singing the last two lines.*

Long pause.

Debbie   Jack.

Pause.

Jack . . .

Jack   I mean, it's not as if we had any . . .

Debbie   Suspicions.

Jack   It's not like we had any doubts . . .

Debbie   We weren't concerned with . . .

Jack   Apart from.

Debbie   Yes.

Jack   The little things.

Debbie   So you say.

Jack   The little things you notice.

Pause.

Habits.

Pause.

Habits.

Debbie   I heard you the first time.

Jack   She's a dreamer.

Debbie   So?

Jack   From the moment they pulled her head out.

Debbie   What?

Jack   They pulled her head out with the forceps and she was never the same since.

Debbie   She . . . ?

Jack   Even the doctor said so.

Debbie   Which doctor?

Jack   The anaesthetist.

Debbie   Who?

Jack   The doctor.

Debbie   I . . .

Jack   She doesn't remember.

Debbie   I don't . . .

Jack   She's fucking out of it, boys, I tell you.

Debbie   Which doctor?

Jack   They clamped her head with the forceps . . .

Debbie   Jack . . .

Jack   They cut you.

Pause.

They cut you . . .

Debbie   No, you're right.

Jack   I know I'm right.

Debbie   She was free.

Jack   What?

Debbie   Free.

Jack   They spread her out on the table and they cut you.

Debbie   She was free, Jack.

Jack   From your hole.

Long pause.

They spread her out on the table . . .

Debbie   Shaking her little fists.

Jack   The head on it.

Debbie Poor darling.

Jack The head . . .

Debbie Her poor misshapen head.

Jack Special needs.

Debbie What?

Jack Abnormal.

Debbie Oh . . .

Jack The junk you feed it.

Debbie Oh, she's special all right.

Jack From your gash.

Debbie Jack . . .

Jack Keep it in your knickers, woman.

Long pause.

Of course you don't notice anything until . . .

Debbie Until it's over.

Pause.

It's not over.

Pause.

It's over.

Jack Debbie . . .

Debbie It's over.

Jack Look . . .

Debbie It's over – listen to her, Jack!

Jack Debbie, please . . .

Debbie I can't stand it any more, I can't . . .

Jack She's just tired.

Debbie   I can't do this.

Jack   Pay no attention . . .

Debbie   Stuck in this house all day . . .

Jack   You're just . . .

Debbie   Stuck with this . . . .

Jack   You're not thinking straight.

Debbie   This fucking thing! . . .

Jack   Even the doctor said so.

Debbie   Listen to her, Jack!

Jack   Most babies . . .

Debbie   I wish she'd just vanish! . . .

Jack   Most babies cry through the night.

Debbie   Stuck on my breast . . .

Jack   Your tit.

Debbie   Draining the very life like some . . .

Jack   Hand her over.

Debbie   Bitch.

Jack   Debbie . . .

Debbie   Deformed little bitch.

Jack   Debbie, please . . .

Debbie   I hope you choke on it.

Pause.

Did I say that out loud?

Pause.

Oh, poor mite.

Jack   Hand her over.

Pause.

Debbie . . .

Debbie   You're doing it on purpose.

Jack   Let me help you.

Debbie   It only to shut her up.

Jack   You're not . . .

Debbie   If only for a moment's peace.

Jack   You can't keep . . .

Debbie   The neighbours, Jack!

Jack   Who?

Debbie   Think of the neighbours.

Jack   Fuck the neighbours.

Debbie   What will they think?

Jack   Most babies . . .

Debbie   What will they think?

Jack   They make an effort, Debbie.

Debbie   Do they?

Jack   They make themselves heard, it's only natural.

Pause.

Come on now, let's . . .

Debbie   Of course we're fine.

Jack   What?

Debbie   We're fine, aren't we, Jack?

Jack   They say it's common.

Debbie   Right.

Jack   The first three months are always hard . . .

Debbie   But after that.

Jack   After that, yes.

Debbie   You should pop over for lunch one day.

Jack   Oh, definitely.

Debbie   Sunday lunch.

Jack   She'd love to meet you.

Debbie   I'll be back at work soon.

Jack   I mean, she's not really . . .

Debbie   Childcare.

Jack   She's not exactly . . .

Debbie   I mean, we don't feel any different, do we?

Jack   No.

Debbie   We're still the same old . . .

Jack   Same old, same old.

Debbie   It's not like you have to stop coming to visit.

Jack   An extra pair of hands, that's all.

Debbie   She's adorable.

Jack   She'll be in her own room soon.

Debbie   You will come and visit us, won't you?

Long pause.

Jack   Debbie . . .

Debbie   I suppose had she been a boy.

Jack   What?

Debbie   Had she been a boy with golden hair. Had she taken after her father. Had she been more . . .

Jack   Had she shown some interest, at least.

Debbie   Had she . . .

Jack   The junk you feed her.

Debbie   Had she been a boy.

Jack   Mars bars and fucking Monster Munch.

Debbie   So it's my fault?

Jack   You should smell that toilet after she's used it for Christ knows what.

Debbie   Her grades, Jack.

Jack   What?

Debbie   Her grades. She has good grades.

Jack   She has average grades.

Debbie   I mean, she's no prodigy.

Jack   Average.

Debbie   She's no freak of fucking nature.

Jack   She's an average student.

Debbie   For her age.

Jack   For any age.

Debbie   She's the youngest in her year.

Jack   She can barely fit into her . . . .

Debbie   Jack. My partner, Jack. He thinks she's retarded.

Jack   The junk you feed her.

Debbie   He thinks.

Jack   Mars bars and fucking Monster Munch.

Debbie   Small wonder they're so jealous. She's with her friends at the bus stop. Of course they're jealous of her grades . . .

Jack   Her average grades.

Debbie   They're talking and laughing and whispering in one another's ears.

Jack   They're pushing each other around.

Debbie   Her friends.

Jack   They're of that age.

Debbie   There's Peggy and Rachel and Richard, and they call to her from the shelter.

Jack   'It's gone half past, Kim!'

Debbie   They're going to be in so much trouble.

Jack   'Kimberly!'

Debbie   Peggy, Rachel and Richard . . .

Jack   'Come on now, hurry!'

Debbie   They're going to get drenched.

Jack   'Get a move on, will you?!'

Debbie   Drenched.

Jack   'Stupid fat cow!'

Debbie   She's got her umbrella and she's so popular now.

Jack   For an average girl.

Debbie   They're so jealous and she's so popular and they're whispering in one another's ears.

Jack   They're whispering about her.

Debbie   No, they . . .

Jack   They're whispering about her.

Debbie   Jack . . .

Jack   I mean, who can fucking blame them, eh?

Debbie   You've left already.

Jack   I . . .

Debbie   You've gone, Jack.

Pause.

You've gone.

Jack   Fine.

Debbie   I change the channels and they're going to be in so much trouble by the time they actually get there. She opens up her brolly and the four of them huddle up. The rain's beating down around them . . .

Jack   What's the time?

Debbie   They don't care what time it is, they're . . .

Jack   'Stupid fat cow, look at her.'

Debbie   'Remedial.'

Jack   'Waddling like a penguin.'

Debbie   'Take her bag.'

Jack   'What?'

Debbie   'Take her bag, Richard, go on.'

Jack   'Wipe my bum with it, you mean?'

Debbie   'Throw it into the road.'

Jack   'Oh . . . '

Debbie   'Throw it under the bus.'

Jack   'Throw her under the bus.'

Debbie   'Stupid fat cow.'

Jack   'Blubber mountain, can't put two sentences together.'

Debbie   'Give me the scissors.'

Jack   'What?'

Debbie   'Ask Mrs Stephens for the scissors, go on.'

Jack   'Cut her hair off?'

Debbie   'Cut her fat off.'

Jack   'You're cruel.'

Debbie   'Puncture her belly.'

Jack   'Her head.'

Debbie   'Cut open her hole, snip snip snip.'

Jack   'Snip, snip, snip!'

Debbie   'Take her piggy eyes out, go on!'

Jack   Who can blame them, eh?

Debbie   Turn it up, Jack, please!

Long pause.

'Richard and Judy'.

Pause.

Jack   Debbie . . .

Debbie   'Friends'.

Pause.

'America's Next Top . . .'

Jack   What's she wearing?

Long pause.

Debbie *and* **Jack**   What's she wearing?

Pause.

Jack   Debbie . . .

Debbie   I forgot the . . .

Jack   What?

Debbie   I forgot the thing, the . . .

Pause.

I forgot to set the . . .

Long pause.

Of course the bus doesn't come.

Pause.

The driver, the bus driver. He forgets.

Jack Right.

Debbie He forgot to set the . . .

Pause.

The thing, the . . .

Jack Have you called them?

Debbie The thing, he forgets to set the . . .

Jack Are you going to just fucking sit there?!

Long pause.

She turns the corner . . .

Pause.

She was late, I was running late.

Pause.

You were carrying on as normal.

Pause.

Debbie . . .

Debbie 'Someone's got the wind in his sails.'

Jack What?

Debbie That's what I thought. 'Someone's in an awful hurry this morning.'

Pause.

'Someone's got the itch.'

Jack Now, look . . .

Debbie   'Where's he off to so early?' I thought.

Jack   Let's not get carried away.

Debbie   'With a twinkle in his eye.'

Jack   Oh, come on . . .

Debbie   With a twinkle in your eye.

Pause.

With a twinkle . . .

Jack   She was late, I was running late.

Debbie   Dirty slut.

Jack   I get up at the same time every morning. I go to the bathroom, have a wash, brush my teeth. I return via the landing to the bedroom and I take my clothes that are laying neatly on the top of the chest of drawers. Of course, I used to wear a suit to work when I was just an apprentice, back in the day. Back in the day, Christ, I must have got over two dozen suits locked away in that fucking wardrobe of mine. I mean, they're good suits, give or take, I think they're partly responsible for getting me to where I am today, fucking shallow bastard management. Though now I'm virtually running the place, well, I can wear whatever I fucking feel like, can't I? I could go dressed as King fucking Kong for all they fucking care.

Debbie   Does she whisper in your ear?

Jack   What?

Debbie   Does she call out your name, Jack?

Jack   Though I still take pride in my appearance, don't get me wrong.

Debbie   Jack . . .

Jack   I have it ironed and folded on the top of the chest of drawers by eight o'clock each night. It only takes me about ten minutes to be up and ready to leave by the time that fucking alarm clock goes off, so I go to the bathroom, have a wash . . .

Debbie   Does she ask about me?

Jack   Look . . .

Debbie   Does she even know?

Pause.

Jack . . .

Jack   I go to the bathroom, have a wash – I'm out the fucking door by half past eight. I'm out the door and I'm behind the wheel and the sun's beating down through the windscreen. Of course, on a good day I might pop into the gym for an hour, this is only on a good day mind, if there's no poor bastard waiting to get sacked or some gobshite from IT needs to reinstall the fucking hard drive for the third time in two months – then I might consider it, right? Twenty minutes on the cross-trainer, a few weights – work up the abdominals, you know? I mean, a man's to keep his figure, hasn't he? A man's got to make the most of what he's got. You don't get to where I am looking like a fucking Neanderthal, d'you know what I mean? You have to stay positive, right? You have to think positive, you have to . . .

Debbie   Does she whisper sweet nothings?

Jack   You have to think positive, Debbie.

Pause.

Go to the gym.

Pause.

Fold the clothes and place them on top of the chest of drawers.

Pause.

Debbie.

Pause.

Fold and place them on . . .

Debbie   She shuts the door behind her and turns the corner at the end of street. Of course, there was no news at that time.

Jack   Of course.

Debbie   There wasn't any . . .

Jack   I mean, don't get me wrong, it's not like I haven't been there, you know? It's not as if I don't . . .

Debbie   At the start.

Jack   At the start, that's right.

Pause.

Watching her grow.

Pause.

The first time she smiled.

Pause.

The first time she called me by my name.

Pause.

Dressing her up. Her little pink outfits.

Debbie   Her dresses.

Jack   Her socks and little mittens.

Debbie   Her sweet winter hat.

Jack   Dressed up and out to meet her friends.

Debbie   All her little parties.

Jack   And everyone pawing over her . . .

Debbie   The neighbours.

Jack   Everyone . . .

Debbie   Next door.

Jack   Her fucking grandparents.

Debbie   The neighbours, Jack.

Jack   In her little winter bonnet . . .

Debbie   What will they think?

Pause.

Biting at my nipple . . .

Jack   Hand her over.

Debbie   Draining the very . . .

Jack   Debbie.

Debbie   If only she would / vanish!

Jack   Go back to sleep, will you?!

Long pause.

You were carrying on as normal.

Debbie   Coco Pops. Glass of milk.

Jack   You weren't thinking.

Debbie   An angel.

Jack   What?

Debbie   She turns the corner like an angel and her friends are waiting for her. They're calling over to her, but I forgot to . . .

Jack   Fold and place them on the top of the chest of drawers, that's right. A man needs his routine, Deborah, you can't blame me for that. A man needs reason, there has to be reason to get out of that fucking bed every morning, you have to think positive – the pair of you, fucking bad as each other . . .

Debbie   The thing, the . . .

Jack   We must have reason, Debbie.

Pause.

We must have reason.

Long pause.

She left for school as normal.

Pause.

She has her breakfast . . .

Debbie   'Bargain Hunt'.

Jack   What?

Debbie   'Bargain Hunt', the programme.

Pause.

The programme . . .

Jack   I wouldn't know.

Debbie   You'd left already.

Jack   Right.

Debbie   'Richard and Judy'.

Pause.

'Friends'.

Pause.

'America's Next Top Model'.

Pause.

'Dad's Army'.

Pause.

'Neighbours'.

Pause.

'The Weakest Link'.

Pause.

'The Simpsons'.

Pause.

'EastEnders', now I like this one. We like this one, don't we, Jack? We like something with a good story.

Pause.

'The Nazis and the Final Solution'.

Pause.

'Celebrity Love Island'.

Pause.

'Newsnight'.

Pause.

'Newsnight'.

Jack   Turn it off, would you?

Debbie   What?

Jack   Go to sleep.

Debbie   Of course, there was no news . . .

Jack   That's enough.

Pause.

Debbie   MTV.

Pause.

The fucking state of that one, look.

Jack   Eminem.

Debbie   Who?

Pause.

Who?

Jack   Blondie bollocks.

Debbie   Oh . . .

Jack   Turn it off, I said.

Debbie   What?

Jack   Turn it off.

Pause.

Well, go on.

Pause.

Go on.

Debbie   It's an old one, look, Jack.

Pause.

Jack, look.

Jack   Right.

Debbie   You know, I haven't seen this one in years. –
What's their name again?

Pause.

Their name, what's their – ? You know the name.

Jack   The Marx Brothers.

Debbie   Who?

Jack   Groucho, Harpo and Chico.

Debbie   What channel is this?

Jack   TCM.

Debbie   Turn it up.

Jack   'Animal Crackers'.

Debbie   What?

Jack   The name of the movie. 'Animal Crackers'.

Debbie   But I can't hear anything.

Jack   You should try and get some sleep.

Debbie   Where is it?

Pause.

Where is it, Jack?

Jack   What?

Debbie   The remote.

Jack   I don't . . .

Debbie   You've hidden the remote.

Jack   I don't have the fucking . . .

Debbie   You're lying on it.

Jack   For Christ's sake . . .

Debbie   Jack!

Jack   Keep your voice down, would you?

Debbie   Pull the cover up.

Jack   What?

Debbie   The quilt.

Jack   You're going to wake her . . .

Debbie   Pull the quilt over your head . . .

Jack   Debbie . . .

Debbie   The quilt, you murdering cunt!

Long pause.

Jack   Debbie . . .

Debbie   Quiet.

Jack   Do you hear?

Pause.

I swear I can hear her, listen.

Long pause.

I can hear her – Debbie.

Pause.

Do you not hear her?

Long pause.

Should I go to see if she's all right?

Pause.

Debbie . . .

Debbie   I'm watching.

Jack   She's got school in a few hours.

Debbie   Then you should have thought of that before.

Jack   What?

Pause.

I should have thought of what before?

Pause.

I should have thought . . . ?

Debbie   Dirty slut.

Pause.

The dirty, filthy slut.

Long pause.

I expect she's blonde.

Pause.

Her blonde hair tumbling over his desk and into the open drawers.

Pause.

Young.

Pause.

Young and free.

Pause.

She's captain of the volleyball team.

Pause.

Has she been cut?

Pause.

Did they cut her open too, Jack?

Jack   Take your clothes off.

Debbie   Right.

Jack   Take your clothes off.

Debbie   That's right.

Jack   Come on.

Debbie   That's perfect.

Jack   You'll catch your death of cold now, get under the covers.

Debbie   And which way would you like it, sir?

Pause.

Would you like to enter from behind?

Jack   Well . . .

Debbie   Might I bend over for you?

Jack   If you like.

Debbie   He says.

Jack   I'd like that, yes.

Debbie   Locking the door.

Jack   That would be very decent of you, Jenny.

Debbie   Her blonde hair tumbling . . .

Jack   You know a man must take care of his physique.

Debbie   Slowly pulling down her knickers.

Jack   Yes, sir.

Debbie   She says.

Jack   Of course, sir.

Debbie   She says.

Jack   Of course.

Debbie   Of course she hasn't been cut, oh no.

Jack   Let me bend over your desk, sir.

Debbie   Her tight neat gash, with her tongue round his pole. Her blonde hair tumbling . . .

Jack   Let me bend over for you.

Debbie   You can tell I've been working out.

Jack   Oh yes, sir.

Debbie   You can feel my biceps.

Jack   Yes . . .

Debbie   Feel my biceps, Jenny.

Jack   Is that better, sir?

Debbie   Deeper.

Jack   It's not too tight for you, I hope.

Debbie   Deeper, come on.

Jack   It's not too tight for you.

Debbie   Her blonde hair tumbling . . .

Jack   It's not too much for you . . .

Debbie   What?

Jack   It's not too . . .

Debbie   What did you just say? It's not too what?

Jack   It's . . . .

Debbie   Not too what-now?

Jack *giggles*.

Debbie   Come on, you just said so –

Jack (*giggles*)   No, don't . . .

Debbie   It's not too . . .

Jack (*giggles*)   Mammy . . .

Debbie   I can't hear you.

Jack (*giggles*)   Mammy, please . . .

Debbie   Is that too tight, sir?

Jack (*giggles*)   Don't . . .

Debbie   Is that too tight for you?

Jack (*giggles*)   Don't tickle . . .

Debbie (*giggles*)   Is that too tight?

Jack (*giggles*)   Please, Mammy . . .

Debbie (*giggles*)   Is that too tight?

Jack (*giggles*)   Stop it, please!

Both laughing.

Pause.

Debbie   Go on now, there's a good girl.

Pause.

You don't want to disappoint Mrs Stephens.

Pause.

Kimberly.

Pause.

You don't want to upset your father now, do you?

Pause.

Well?

Pause.

You don't want to upset anyone.

Pause.

Kimberly.

Pause.

Kimberly, please . . .

Jack   But Daddy said.

Debbie   I don't care what Daddy said.

Jack   But –

Debbie   It's only a silly umbrella, now, come on – the early bird catches what?

Jack   I know.

Debbie   You're late enough as it is.

Jack   Sorry.

Debbie   What?

Jack   I didn't . . .

Debbie   What?

Jack   I didn't mean . . .

Debbie   You've spilt your Coco Pops all down your chin, look.

Jack   Oh.

Debbie   Dirty so-and-so, what are you?

Jack   But I . . .

Debbie   Dirty so-and-so. – Here, let me clean you . . .

Jack   I didn't mean to wake you.

Debbie   What?

Jack   I couldn't sleep, I couldn't . . .

Debbie   Now, daughter . . .

Jack   They were coming for me, Mammy.

Debbie   Now, just . . .

Jack   Daddy told me.

Debbie   He . . . ?

Jack   They were going to swallow me whole. They were tapping at the window, Mammy, he promised.

Debbie   They're just nightmares.

Jack   I know, but –

Debbie   Nightmares, that's all, you were having nightmares.

Jack   But Daddy . . .

Debbie   Daddy nothing.

Jack   Daddy said . . .

Debbie   There's no one coming for you.

Jack   Daddy said I should . . .

Debbie   There's nothing, you hear?

Jack   I should . . .

Debbie   You're going to be late, now . . .

Jack   But I . . .

Debbie   We're running late, come on . . .

Jack   He said I shouldn't bother you.

Debbie   Well, Daddy says a lot of things.

Jack   He told me about the boy . . .

Debbie   Who?

Jack   The golden-haired boy.

Debbie   Look . . .

Jack   He told me the story . . .

Debbie   Daddy doesn't know any boys.

Jack   But . . .

Debbie   Daddy hates boys, you know that.

Jack   In the story . . .

Debbie   He hates boys and little girls.

Jack   On the cloud . . .

Debbie   He's full of hate, Kimberly – Now come on, let's not bicker.

Jack   But . . .

Debbie   I'm your mother, look at me.

Jack   I only meant . . .

Debbie   Take sides with him.

Jack   But . . .

Debbie   After all we've been through . . .

Jack   Please . . .

Debbie   I'm your mother, Kimberly, look at me!

Long pause.

What else did he tell you?

Pause.

What did he tell you about me?

Pause.

You know it's wrong to take sides against your mammy.

Pause.

Kimberly.

Pause.

It's a dreadful sin, you know that, don't you?

Pause.

Kimberly . . .

Jack   Turn it down, for Christ's sake.

Debbie   You know you shouldn't listen to that man.

Jack   Go to sleep.

Debbie   You know you shouldn't forget . . .

Jack   Debbie, please . . .

Debbie   I can't forget.

Jack   Just . . .

Debbie   What you've done to her . . .

Jack   What?

Debbie   To us. What you've done to us, you murdering cunt!

Long pause.

'Animal Crackers'.

Pause.

'Bargain Hunt'.

Pause.

'Animal Crackers'.

Jack   Debbie, please . . .

Debbie   Groucho, Harpo and Chico.

Jack   You know she can't sleep . . .

Debbie   'Animal Crackers'.

Jack   Look . . .

Debbie   I've seen this one before, Jack.

Jack   She can't sleep with that noise.

Debbie   I remember now.

Jack   Turn it . . .

Debbie   You remember, don't you, Jack?

Pause.

Jack   Debbie . . .

Debbie   I remember, look.

Long pause.

Jack   Should I go to see if she's all right?

Pause.

Debbie.

Pause.

She's got school in a few hours.

Pause.

She's got school.

Pause.

Should I go and see her?

Pause.

Should I go and tuck her in?

Pause.

I'd like that.

Pause.

I could tell her a bedtime story, couldn't I, Debbie?

Pause.

I could do that.

Pause.

I can hear her.

Pause.

Debbie.

Pause.

Tell me you can hear her.

Pause.

Debbie, please.

Pause.

Come with me.

Long pause.

Come with me, we can take the car. We can see if she's still out there . . .

Debbie   . . . with the sun beating down.

Jack Debbie . . .

Debbie You remember, don't you, Jack?

Jack Look at me . . .

Debbie And at such . . .

Jack You've called the school, I hope.

Pause.

You called the school at least.

Pause.

You called the school.

Long pause.

Are you going to just fucking sit there?!

Long pause.

Debbie And at such a young age.

Jack Please . . .

Debbie Hidden in the bushes, with the sun beating down.

Jack Debbie . . .

Debbie You remember, Jack. The two of us.

Long pause.

As before, she sings the chorus of 'La Isla Bonita'.

Pause.

She and **Jack** *sing the middle eight / bridge of the song – beginning 'I want to be . . .' and ending with '. . . a girl loves a boy'.*

Long pause.

Debbie   There's someone out there.

Pause.

There's someone out there, Jack.

Pause.

There's some *thing* out there.

Long pause.

She has her breakfast.

Pause.

She turns the corner, I switch on the news. Of course, there was no news, not at that time, not on the terrestrial channel.

Jack   You're late.

Debbie   She's late and she crosses the street to the shelter.

Pause.

There's no one there. Her friends, her jealous friends, they . . .

Jack   They forget.

Debbie   She's too good for them, she's too good – even the doctor said so. The doctor said nothing when he saw her grades, and so she waits. She waits with the rain – the sun – with the sun pouring down – The sun's pouring down and the days are getting shorter, she waits.

Pause.

Jack   There's nothing . . .

Debbie   There's no one around for miles, they forget –

They all forget and she's out there all alone. She's out there under the shelter, her umbrella in her bag. The sun's pouring down, but she won't . . .

Pause.

She's a good girl.

Pause.

She's a good girl and they know it. They know it, the bastards. The bastards, the three of them. The three of them watching from the bushes, they can see her now, the monsters, the dirty monsters. They're creeping out under the bushes and they don't take their eyes off her, poor girl.

Jack   Poor girl.

Debbie   Poor misshapen girl.

Jack   Right.

Debbie   Poor angel with the three. They see her under the shelter and they creep up the path behind her. Whispering. Whispering in her ear.

Jack   Groucho, Harpo and Chico.

Debbie   They take her away.

Pause.

They take her out the shelter, they lead her up the hill. They fill her pockets with sweets and lead her up the hill. Huddled up and holding hands, they take her up up over and then they pass the school – Pass the school, past the gate and she says, she says . . . 'But Mammy said,' she says, and they laugh, and the first one says something funny out the corner and now they laugh, they're all laughing. They're laughing so hard and the quiet one honks his horn, and she's raised up on his back and it's horses, playing horses. Clippity-clop clippity-clop, all the while honking – past the school, past the shops, and down behind the houses. 'School? What school? Didn't your daddy tell you? Didn't your mammy say?' – with the rain, with the sun, with the sun blistering their cheeks. They laugh and they gallop and there's no one else for miles.

Jack You lose an hour.

Debbie You lose an hour, and they take her back inside. Inside their room with no doors, the room has no doors.

Jack A window?

Debbie No window. Just a shelf with a towel and they place her on the floor. The dark one lights his cigar, while the others dry her off. They take her bag and her umbrella and she says . . . 'But Mammy said,' she says, and all the time they're laughing – all the time they're laughing – Place her on the floor, cross-legged, and dry her down before the rain. They fight amongst her clothes, and the quiet one takes his scissors, the small one feeds her peanuts, while the dark one blows thick smoke. No doors, no windows, and there's no one else for miles. They're pointing with the scissors, and laughing, snip snip snip.

Pause.

They're laughing, snip snip snip.

Jack Monsters.

Debbie Filthy monsters.

Pause.

That's right.

Pause.

That's right, the dirty devils, and they're wading in her blood, they're wading in our angel and she's drowning in their dirt. And they're whispering in their ears, and the ticking of the clock. Past the school, past the houses and they're knocking down the doors. They're smashing through the windows, and they're pulling up the floors. They're ripping all the signs down and sweeping up the tills. The school bell from the school bell and the shelter from the stop. The bus spins up and

over, and the driver's way ahead, through the windshield . . .
Through the windshield and the channels all dead. 'All dead,'
cry the others, they're screaming now, they're screaming. The
blood the flood and the mothers clinging to the trees. 'But
Mammy said,' they scream, with the ticking down the hour,
and the sun for miles ahead. 'Jesus, save us,' goes the cry.
'Jesus wept for all mankind.' But the devils lose their patience
and they're snipping at the tongues, they're snipping at the
holes. They're snipping at the doctors, the drivers, the blondes,
they're snipping at her soul – her poor misshapen soul.
They're snipping at the schoolyard, and they're packing up
the clothes. Her blonde hair burns like bonfire, and the breasts
all turn and wilt. The grades dry up in season, and
prescriptions turn to ghosts. Channel-hopping, the floor
they're mopping, laughing and twisting and spinning to the
grave – 'Jesus save us,' they're praying. 'Jesus stay!'

Pause.

Jack   And sure enough . . .

Pause.

And sure enough . . .

Debbie   A boy.

Jack   That's right.

Debbie   A golden-haired boy.

Pause.

That's right, on the hour. On the back of a cloud.

Jack   Seated.

Debbie   Seated on the back of a dark distant cloud.

Long pause.

I told you to take your umbrella.

Pause.

What did I say?

Jack　The rain.

Debbie　The weather forecast's rain.

Jack　There's a good girl.

Debbie　A good girl.

Pause.

The rain washes everything away.

Long pause.

I switch on the news, she turns the corner.

Long pause.

She turns the corner.

Jack　Turn it off now, go to sleep.

Debbie　I told you to take your umbrella.

Jack　Put your head down.

Pause.

Go to sleep, go on.

Pause.

We've got to be up early.

Pause.

Well?

Pause.

What do we say?

Pause.

The early bird catches what?

Pause.

The early bird catches what?

Blackout.

Methuen Drama Contemporary Dramatists

include

John Arden (two volumes)
Arden & D'Arcy
Peter Barnes (three volumes)
Sebastian Barry
Dermot Bolger
Edward Bond (eight volumes)
Howard Brenton
  (two volumes)
Richard Cameron
Jim Cartwright
Caryl Churchill (two volumes)
Sarah Daniels (two volumes)
Nick Darke
David Edgar (three volumes)
David Eldridge
Ben Elton
Dario Fo (two volumes)
Michael Frayn (three volumes)
John Godber (three volumes)
Paul Godfrey
David Greig
John Guare
Lee Hall (two volumes)
Peter Handke
Jonathan Harvey
  (two volumes)
Declan Hughes
Terry Johnson (three volumes)
Sarah Kane
Barrie Keefe
Bernard-Marie Koltès
  (two volumes)
Franz Xaver Kroetz
David Lan
Bryony Lavery
Deborah Levy
Doug Lucie

David Mamet (four volumes)
Martin McDonagh
Duncan McLean
Anthony Minghella
  (two volumes)
Tom Murphy (five volumes)
Phyllis Nagy
Anthony Neilson
Philip Osment
Gary Owen
Louise Page
Stewart Parker (two volumes)
Joe Penhall
Stephen Poliakoff
  (three volumes)
David Rabe
Mark Ravenhill
Christina Reid
Philip Ridley
Willy Russell
Eric-Emmanuel Schmitt
Ntozake Shange
Sam Shepard (two volumes)
Wole Soyinka (two volumes)
Simon Stephens
Shelagh Stephenson
David Storey (three volumes)
Sue Townsend
Judy Upton
Michel Vinaver
  (two volumes)
Arnold Wesker (two volumes)
Michael Wilcox
Roy Williams (two volumes)
Snoo Wilson (two volumes)
David Wood (two volumes)
Victoria Wood

Methuen Drama World Classics

include

Jean Anouilh (two volumes)
Brendan Behan
Aphra Behn
Bertolt Brecht (eight volumes)
Büchner
Bulgakov
Calderón
Čapek
Anton Chekhov
Noël Coward (eight volumes)
Feydeau
Eduardo De Filippo
Max Frisch
John Galsworthy
Gogol
Gorky (two volumes)
Harley Granville Barker
  (two volumes)
Victor Hugo
Henrik Ibsen (six volumes)
Jarry

Lorca (three volumes)
Marivaux
Mustapha Matura
David Mercer (two volumes)
Arthur Miller (five volumes)
Molière
Musset
Peter Nichols (two volumes)
Joe Orton
A. W. Pinero
Luigi Pirandello
Terence Rattigan
  (two volumes)
W. Somerset Maugham
  (two volumes)
August Strindberg
  (three volumes)
J. M. Synge
Ramón del Valle-Inclán
Frank Wedekind
Oscar Wilde

Methuen Drama Classical Greek Dramatists

Aeschylus Plays: One
(Persians, Seven Against Thebes, Suppliants,
Prometheus Bound)

Aeschylus Plays: Two
(Oresteia: Agamemnon, Libation-Bearers, Eumenides)

Aristophanes Plays: One
(Acharnians, Knights, Peace, Lysistrata)

Aristophanes Plays: Two
(Wasps, Clouds, Birds, Festival Time, Frogs)

Aristophanes & Menander: New Comedy
(Women in Power, Wealth, The Malcontent,
The Woman from Samos)

Euripides Plays: One
(Medea, The Phoenician Women, Bacchae)

Euripides Plays: Two
(Hecuba, The Women of Troy, Iphigeneia at Aulis,
Cyclops)

Euripides Plays: Three
(Alkestis, Helen, Ion)

Euripides Plays: Four
(Elektra, Orestes, Iphigeneia in Tauris)

Euripides Plays: Five
(Andromache, Herakles' Children, Herakles)

Euripides Plays: Six
(Hippolytos, Suppliants, Rhesos)

Sophocles Plays: One
(Oedipus the King, Oedipus at Colonus, Antigone)

Sophocles Plays: Two
(Ajax, Women of Trachis, Electra, Philoctetes)

Methuen Drama Modern Plays

include work by

Edward Albee
Jean Anouilh
John Arden
Margaretta D'Arcy
Peter Barnes
Sebastian Barry
Brendan Behan
Dermot Bolger
Edward Bond
Bertolt Brecht
Howard Brenton
Anthony Burgess
Simon Burke
Jim Cartwright
Caryl Churchill
Complicite
Noël Coward
Lucinda Coxon
Sarah Daniels
Nick Darke
Nick Dear
Shelagh Delaney
David Edgar
David Eldridge
Dario Fo
Michael Frayn
John Godber
Paul Godfrey
David Greig
John Guare
Peter Handke
David Harrower
Jonathan Harvey
Iain Heggie
Declan Hughes
Terry Johnson
Sarah Kane
Charlotte Keatley
Barrie Keeffe

Howard Korder
Robert Lepage
Doug Lucie
Martin McDonagh
John McGrath
Terrence McNally
David Mamet
Patrick Marber
Arthur Miller
Mtwa, Ngema & Simon
Tom Murphy
Phyllis Nagy
Peter Nichols
Sean O'Brien
Joseph O'Connor
Joe Orton
Louise Page
Joe Penhall
Luigi Pirandello
Stephen Poliakoff
Franca Rame
Mark Ravenhill
Philip Ridley
Reginald Rose
Willy Russell
Jean-Paul Sartre
Sam Shepard
Wole Soyinka
Simon Stephens
Shelagh Stephenson
Peter Straughan
C. P. Taylor
Theatre Workshop
Sue Townsend
Judy Upton
Timberlake Wertenbaker
Roy Williams
Snoo Wilson
Victoria Wood

Methuen Drama Student Editions

Jean Anouilh *Antigone* • John Arden *Serjeant Musgrave's Dance* • Alan Ayckbourn *Confusions* • Aphra Behn *The Rover* • Edward Bond *Lear* • Bertolt Brecht *The Caucasian Chalk Circle* • *Life of Galileo* • *Mother Courage and her Children* • *The Resistible Rise of Arturo Ui* • *The Threepenny Opera* • Anton Chekhov *The Cherry Orchard* • *The Seagull* • *Three Sisters* • *Uncle Vanya* • Caryl Churchill *Serious Money* • *Top Girls* • Shelagh Delaney *A Taste of Honey* • Euripides *Elektra* • *Medea* • Dario Fo *Accidental Death of an Anarchist* • Michael Frayn *Copenhagen* • John Galsworthy *Strife* • Nikolai Gogol *The Government Inspector* • Robert Holman *Across Oka* • Henrik Ibsen *A Doll's House* • *Hedda Gabler* • Charlotte Keatley *My Mother Said I Never Should* • Bernard Kops *Dreams of Anne Frank* • Federico García Lorca *Blood Wedding* • *The House of Bernarda Alba* (bilingual edition) • *Yerma* (bilingual edition) • David Mamet *Glengarry Glen Ross* • *Oleanna* • Patrick Marber *Closer* • Joe Orton *Loot* • Luigi Pirandello *Six Characters in Search of an Author* • Mark Ravenhill *Shopping and F***ing* • Willy Russell *Blood Brothers* • Sophocles *Antigone* • Wole Soyinka *Death and the King's Horseman* • August Strindberg *Miss Julie* • J. M. Synge *The Playboy of the Western World* • Theatre Workshop *Oh What a Lovely War* • Timberlake Wertenbaker *Our Country's Good* • Arnold Wesker *The Merchant* • Oscar Wilde *The Importance of Being Earnest* • Tennessee Williams *A Streetcar Named Desire* • *The Glass Menagerie*